THE WORLD RECORD

REVISED & EXPANDED

PAPER AIRPLANE BOOK

Text by Ken Blackburn

Plane Designs by
Ken Blackburn & Jeff Lammers

WORKMAN PUBLISHING, NEW YORK

To Paul and Lynn Blackburn for their love and encouragement, for teaching me to be persistent, hardworking, and an original thinker, and for their good genes which resulted in a strong arm. I would also like to thank my wife, Lauren, for her assistance, understanding, and for putting up with a husband who refuses to grow up. —KB

Thanks to all our faithful PAPs (Paper Airplane Pilots) who have made this book so successful over the years. I am particularly grateful to my wife, Karen, and my newest test pilot, Melissa. —JL

Library of Congress Cataloging-in-Publication Data is available
ISBN-10: 0-7611-4383-1
ISBN-13: 978-0-7611-4383-3

Illustrations by David Allen
Photographs by Tod Seelie and Jenna Bascom. Photographs on page 9 and 10 by Peloton Sports. Photograph of the Space Shuttle on page 15 by Antique Research Center/TIPS Images. Eagle, Hammerhead, Stunt, and World Record Paper Airplane by Mark Reidy. Vortex, Falcon, Interceptor, and Galactica by Shi Chen. Metropolis, Chopper, and Camel by Michael Fusco. Phantom and Shuttle by Don Hillenbrand. Stiletto and Flying Wing by Robert Zimmerman. Basic Dart and Valkyrie by Orlando Adiao. Spitfire by Mark Monlux. Basic Square Plane by David Riedy. Stratus by Flamur Tonuzi.

Workman books are available at a special discount when purchased in bulk for special premiums and sales promotions as well as for fund-raising or educational use. Special editions or book excerpts can also be created to specification. For details, contact the Special Sales Director at the address below.

Workman Publishing Company, Inc.
225 Varick Street
New York, NY 10014-4381

Manufactured in the United States of America

First printing October 2006
10 9 8 7 6 5 4 3 2 1

Contents

TEST YOUR ACCURACY WITH THE RUNWAY, LOCATED BETWEEN THE FLIGHT LOG AND THE HANGAR.

History of the World Record Paper Airplane

WHEN I WAS ABOUT EIGHT years old, I made one of my frequent trips to the aviation section of the library in Kernersville, North Carolina, and checked out a book that included instructions for a simple square paper airplane. I found that it flew better than the paper darts I was used to making. Thrown straight up, it reached much higher altitudes.

To the dismay of my teachers, I folded many of these planes, experimenting with changes to the original design. (One of the beauties of paper airplanes is that they are perfectly suited to trial and error testing. If one doesn't work, it's cheap and easy to start over.) One of my designs would level off at the peak of

The Basic Square

The Basic Dart

its climb and then start a slow downward glide. Sometimes, with the help of rising air currents, I achieved flights lasting nearly a minute and covering about 1,000 feet.

In 1977, I received a *Guinness Book of World Records* as a gift. Naturally the first thing I turned to was the aviation section. The paper airplane "time aloft" record was 15 seconds, set by William Pryor in 1975. It dawned on me that my planes (without help from the wind) were flying at close to world record times. On my next outing, I timed the best flights. They weren't quite long enough to break the record, but with a little work I thought I could do it.

With this goal in mind, I refined my

plane designs and worked on my throw. Many people are surprised to learn that I consider the throw to be almost as important as the plane itself. The faster the throw, the higher the airplane goes and, therefore, the longer the flight.

In 1979, when I was a junior in high school, I made an official attempt at the world record. The record was described in the *Guinness Book* as time "over level ground," so I chose the school's baseball field as my staging ground. One afternoon, with my teachers as timers and a reporter on hand from the *Winston-Salem Journal,* I let my favorite square plane fly. With the help of the wind, I made a flight of 24.9 seconds, and was sure I had flown right into the pages of history.

The World Record Paper Airplane

Unfortunately, the letter I received back from Guinness Superlatives, Ltd., wasn't quite what I had hoped for. They informed me that the flight had to be performed indoors.

The next year, I worked part-time at Reynolds Coliseum in Winston-Salem, parking cars and moving equipment. In my time off, I had access to the largest indoor paper airplane practice arena I would ever need. My best flights yielded times of over 17 seconds, and I knew the record was mine for the taking, but I got sidetracked by college applications.

A Second Attempt

August of 1981 was the beginning of four years of aerospace engineering at North Carolina State University. I lived on the sixth then the eighth floor, perfect airplane launching pads (even though throwing objects from dorm windows was strictly prohibited). I made planes from every paper product available—from pizza boxes to computer punch cards—in many bizarre shapes, and soon infected the dorm with plane-flying fever.

Still, it wasn't until my junior year that my friends began encouraging me to make another stab at the world record, and I finally decided to give it a try. I practiced several times at the school coliseum, keeping the best plane from my sessions, nicknamed "Old Bossy," for the record attempt. Old Bossy was regularly achieving times over 17 seconds, well above the 15-second record.

A friend arranged for a reporter from the school newspaper to meet us at the coliseum. I made a few warm-up throws, and then reached for Old Bossy. With a mighty heave, I sent the plane hurtling into the upper reaches of the coliseum . . . and directly into a cluster of speakers near the ceiling. I was devastated. My best plane, Old Bossy, gone forever.

My roommate handed me a piece of ordinary copier paper and I quickly made another airplane. My second throw with the new plane was the best of the afternoon at 16.89 seconds. It beat the old record, but I knew I could have done better with Old Bossy. I sent Guinness the newspaper article, signatures of the witnesses, and Old Bossy's replacement. This time Guinness responded with the letter I'd been waiting for.

After graduation, I went to work for an aerospace company— McDonnell Douglas in St. Louis, Missouri. In the summer of 1987, I was finishing a job on the F-18 Hornet, when I got an unexpected call from California. A television production company was putting

1985 GUINNESS BOOK OF WORLD RECORDS

Paper Airplane

The flight duration for a paper aircraft over level ground is 16.89 sec by Ken Blackburn in the Reynolds Coliseum at NC State Univ, Raleigh, on Nov 29, 1983.

together a series featuring people attempting to break world records. Would I be interested in trying to reset my record? I didn't have to think long before replying with a definite yes. The filming was only a few weeks away and I usually needed at least a month to get my throwing arm in shape, so I started practicing immediately.

Round Three

With my best practice airplanes packed in an old shoe box, I set out on my all-expense-paid extravaganza to Milwaukee. It turned out that Tony Feltch, the distance record holder for paper airplanes, was also there, trying to beat his record, and that we'd be making our attempts in the Milwaukee Convention Center.

Tony went first and, after only a few throws, broke his old record, achieving a distance of nearly 200 feet. Additional filming and interviews with Tony dragged on for hours, leaving me on the sidelines, sweating bullets.

Finally, it was my turn. I picked out my best plane from practice, and got the nod from the producer that the cameras were rolling. I heaved the airplane upward, and watched it float down. The official called out a time of 15.02 seconds. I concentrated harder on my second throw, but was again rewarded with a time of only 15.47 seconds. Suddenly it struck me that I might not be able to reset the record. Even in good condition, my arm lasts for only a couple of world record throws in any one day.

I made my third throw with everything I had. (I estimate that these throws leave my hand at a speed close to 60 miles an hour.) The launch seemed better, but the stopwatch would be the final judge.

As the plane came to a smooth silent landing on the floor, the official yelled out, "17.20 seconds!" Yes, a new world record! I made two more throws, but neither beat the record.

Another Chance

For a little while after my segment aired I felt like a celebrity. Friends and relatives called me, and kids in my neighborhood wanted me to autograph paper airplanes. But the excitement soon died down, and I went back to my normal life. Still, I continued modifying and flying my paper airplanes. In 1990, I fine-tuned my planes, built up my arm, and achieved several 20-second flights (which, of course, no one was around to see, much less officially record).

In 1994, I received another surprise

call from a TV program; this time it was from a British show called *Record Breakers*. They wanted to know if I'd be willing to reset the world record again in a month in New York City. I enthusiastically agreed and immediately started working out in preparation. I was fortunate enough to find a trainer who was also the pitcher for a college baseball team and could help me strengthen my 30-year-old arm.

February 17 found me standing next to an enormous DC-10 in American Airlines Hangar Number 10 at JFK Airport, the chosen place for the attempt. I walked up to the plane and looked in awe at the 200-foot-long, 100-million-dollar backdrop for my 5-inch-long folded piece of paper. I had an enthusiastic crowd of onlookers consisting of the hangar's maintenance crew and other personnel, all waiting to see the world record broken.

The cameras began to roll. I felt confident, but more nervous than I'd expected. My first throw bombed as a result of a poor launch. During my second throw, I concentrated on good form, giving it everything I had to offer. The launch felt a lot better. The plane started a slow turn to the left, narrowly avoiding a collision with the DC-10's tail. I could tell it was a good flight, but only the timer would know exactly how good.

When he called out 18.8 seconds, everyone began to clap. I had forgotten the thrill of setting a record, and was running on adrenaline for hours afterward.

Surpassed—Briefly

In 1996 the BBC invited me to try to reset my record, this time on live TV in London with 20 other teams competing. I won the contest with a flight time of 17.3 seconds, but unbeknownst to me, after the event two of the other contestants, Chris Edge and Andy Currey, continued working on their planes and set a new record of 20.9 seconds on July 28, 1996. The record did not appear in the *Guinness Book* until the 1998 edition. That January, I glanced through a freshly printed copy and discovered to my horror that I had been displaced. I had to get my record back.

I knew it would take at least six months of daily preparation to have a chance of resetting the record. My plan was to construct and test between five and ten planes a week. Initially, I tried radical changes to my design, progressively narrowing in on the best paper airplane design for a record attempt. I also started working with a

professional athletic trainer, Dorri Buckholtz, focusing on strengthening my arm. She was extremely helpful, giving me detailed instructions for exercises designed to improve my throwing speed.

Despite my new designs, I had the most luck with the original model I'd invented as a kid (the one that's included in this book). But I did find a few ways to make the plane fly better and more consistently. First, it's important to keep the folds as flat as possible, which I did by pressing each fold with the side of a pen as I constructed the plane. Second, I experimented with making the folds both a little wider and a little narrower until I found just the right width. Third, I added crease marks on the wings which, like the dimples on a golf ball, reduced drag.

I started by practicing indoors in order to get consistent flying times. My primary flying site was a large assembly area at Boeing—where I'd also practiced for my 1994 and 1996 records—but I quickly ran into problems. It was being used for the final assembly of the navy's newest fighter, the F/A-18E/F, which meant there wasn't enough space, and the 60-foot ceilings were also proving to be too low. My best flights often hit the ceiling, and I lost some of my best planes forever when they lodged on top of beams or ventilation ducts. So I began practicing outside, but weather and air currents made it difficult to determine the exact flight performance of each plane.

1996 GUINNESS BOOK OF WORLD RECORDS

Paper Airplane

The flight duration for a paper aircraft over level ground is 18.80 sec by Ken Blackburn at American Airlines Hangar 10, JFK Airport, Queens, NY, Feb 17, 1994.

I knew my best planes were flying just over 20 seconds, but by how much?

Finding a facility for attempting the record was another challenge. Through the help of a family friend, I eventually secured the Georgia Dome (home of the Atlanta Falcons), and a date of October 8th, 1998, was set. Not only did I have a facility of my dreams, but the staff also agreed to give me an extra day in the dome to practice before I attempted the record!

Atlanta

Guinness requires media coverage, videotape, and photographs, as well as the record corroborated by two designated officials known as "Scrutineers."

The world record throw, 1998

Organizing all this at a location 500 miles from home was quite a challenge, but with the help of my sister, Jackie Tyson, and the publisher of this book, everything came together—now all I had to do was go ahead and set the record!

Wednesday, October 7th, was my practice day. Words can't describe how overwhelming it was to have one of the largest rooms in the world silent and still, just for me! But there was one problem.

It was raining, and with the dome's ventilation turned off, the humidity had filtered indoors as well. It wasn't a complete showstopper, but it was affecting my planes. After an hour of testing, only two planes had flown beyond the existing record, and both by less than a second! By the end of the day, I was somewhat satisfied I could break the record, but only if the humidity didn't increase further.

Thursday, October 8th, started out cloudy and very humid. I grabbed my Rubbermaid containers (Rubbermaid makes a great waterproof, crushproof paper airplane hangar) and headed down to the Georgia Dome.

As I approached the dome, the clouds appeared to be lifting, so I hoped the humidity wouldn't be a problem. When I walked indoors, both CNN and the local news crews were there to greet me. I made some practice throws to warm up my arm and to allow the media some close-up views of my launch. While I waited for everyone else to arrive, I met the Scrutineers, went over the rules, and showed them my planes. Then it was show time.

The Final Attempt

The rules allow just ten official throws, so first I took out my best plane from the day before and fine-tuned it until it flew just right and the practice times exceeded 20 seconds. I made sure the Scrutineers were ready, and I took the field for my first official flight. I gave it my best throw—it flew erratically, but still it looked good. I waited nervously for the official time from the Scrutineers. 21.3 seconds—a new record! What a relief. Nonetheless I decided I would use all my available throws to make sure to get the best time possible. The second throw went straight up—and straight down. After a small adjustment, another good flight, 23.1 seconds! Throw number four was another dud, but number five had a great launch and was 24.2 seconds! Just think, only five minutes earlier I thought I might not be able to beat the record! Throw number six

The Scrutineers and another observer at the Georgia Dome, October 8, 1998

was a dud, and throws seven and eight were both a little short, and throw nine was another dud. This was my last throw—I gave it all I had. This time it was a great throw, and it had a great transition to slow flight. When it landed I knew it was a long flight, but longer than 24.2 seconds? I heard the time as I walked over to retrieve my plane: 27.6 seconds! YES! Better than I had ever hoped or dreamed. With luck, help, and hard work, the summit had been reached!

I submitted the necessary materials to Guinness, and I received notification from them on April 30th, 1999, that my record had become official. I may now be retired from setting records—but who knows what the future might hold.

CURRENT GUINNESS WORLD RECORD

Paper Airplane

The flight duration for a paper aircraft over level ground is 27.6 sec by Ken Blackburn at the Georgia Dome in Atlanta, Oct 8, 1998.

A Whirlwind Tour of Aerodynamics

Why Paper Airplanes Fly

DESPITE MY DEGREE IN AERO-space engineering and many years of work in the field, explaining why a paper airplane stays in the air is not easy. I'll begin by saying that paper airplanes fly using the same general principles as real airplanes. Both are controlled by four basic forces: weight, lift, thrust, and drag. Think of it as two teams each playing tug-of-war with the airplane attached to a rope in the middle.

Weight vs. Lift

The first team, weight and lift, play a vertical game of tug-of-war. Because gravity is constantly trying to pull the airplane to the ground, **WEIGHT** is obviously on the downward side of the rope. **LIFT** exerts an upward pull. As an airplane flies, its wings are angled with the front edges higher than the back edges. This causes the air going over the top of the wings to speed up

slightly as it gets sucked downward across the wing. The air traveling under the wing slows down a bit as it gets shoved by the bottom of the wing. The speeding up and slowing down of the air is what creates lift.

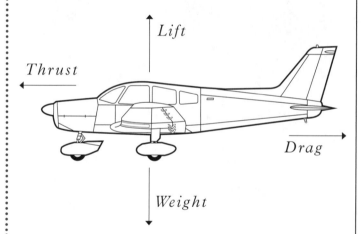

As eighteenth-century Swiss scientist Daniel Bernoulli discovered, when air speeds up its pressure is reduced, and when air slows down its pressure is increased. Therefore the air that speeds up over the top of the wing creates a slight suction that pulls upward on the wing. At the same time, the air below the wing creates extra pressure which pushes upward on the wing. Lift is the combination of these two forces. During straight level flight both lift and weight are pulling equally. If lift pulls harder than weight, the plane begins to accelerate up; if weight pulls harder, the plane accelerates down.

LIFT IN ACTION

Make two simple paper airplanes of the same design. They'll each have just about the same weight, lift, and drag. Now crumple one of the planes into a ball of paper. They still weigh the same, but you have changed the lift and drag.

Hold the paper airplane in one hand, and the paper ball in the other. To the best of your ability, holding one in each hand, throw them at the same level and speed. Which hits the ground first? The paper ball does—it has no lift because it doesn't have wings.

Drag vs. Thrust

While lift and weight are tugging up and down on our airplane, thrust and drag are pulling forward and aft. Let's look at **DRAG** first. When you fly a paper airplane level across a room, drag is what pulls back on your airplane and slows it down. Most of drag comes from air resistance. Thin and insubstantial as air may seem, it does have mass and in some ways is like runny maple syrup. As a plane flies, the air's viscosity makes it stick to the plane, creating resistance to motion. Another source of drag comes from lift: Lift never pulls directly up, but rather tugs up and a little back, and that backward pull contributes to drag.

THRUST is on the opposite end of our imaginary rope, pulling or pushing the plane forward. Real airplanes get their thrust from a propeller or a jet engine. Paper airplanes get it from your arm, then from gravity. A throw gives them their initial speed, and then they fly a little downward, letting gravity pull them along (like a bicycle coasting down a hill).

When you throw a paper airplane from a building or hill, the plane descends at an angle that allows gravity to balance the pull of drag, so the plane won't slow down. A typical paper airplane's drag is about one-fifth its weight. This requires the paper airplane to fly at an angle approximately 11 degrees below level in order for gravity (weight) to pull forward enough to counteract drag.

Why Paper Airplanes Crash

In addition to understanding the forces that affect flight, it's helpful to know some of the properties good airplanes share. Most important is the property we call **STABILITY,** which helps an airplane return to steady flight after a bad throw or a strong gust of wind. An unstable plane will tumble out of control or go into a tight, spiraling dive.

There are three basic types of stability: pitch, directional, and spiral. Pitch stability keeps the airplane's nose from pointing too far up or down. Directional stability keeps an airplane's nose from veering to the right or left. Spiral stability keeps the airplane from spinning or rolling about its body or fuselage.

The first of these, **PITCH STABILITY,** keeps the airplane flying at a constant speed. If the nose of the plane "pitches" up, it will slow down. If it pitches down, it will speed up. There is a small distance along the length of the airplane where it must bal-

DRAG AND WEIGHT

In the late 1500s, Galileo theorized and proved that objects with different weights fall at the same speed. To prove it to yourself, take a quarter and a penny, raise them as high as you can, and drop them at the same time—they should land simultaneously even though the quarter weighs more than twice as much as the penny.

All objects fall to earth at the same speed (actually, at the same acceleration) because of the force of gravity. But when you add drag into the equation, things change. Say, you drop a penny and a feather simultaneously—obviously they won't hit the ground at the same time. This is because of drag. When the force of drag builds up, two objects will then fall at the same rate only if their weights and drag are proportional to each other. For example, if you have two feathers, and one is twice the weight *and* has twice the drag of the other, they will fall at the same rate. This allows us to compare the drag of different objects. If they weigh the same, the one with the most drag lands last. Keep in mind that if the objects are heavy and small, they must fall a long way to build up enough speed for drag to affect their falling speed.

As an experiment, take a few sheets of paper and fold them into a variety of different airplane shapes. Keep one sheet flat. Drop the planes and sheet of paper simultaneously (you may need an extra pair of hands for this) and see which shape falls the fastest and which falls the slowest. Generally, a long and pointed paper airplane when dropped nose down will fall the fastest. Not surprisingly, the flat sheet of paper dropped like a parachute will fall slowest. The higher the drop point, the easier it is to determine the difference in drag.

ance to have the optimum pitch stability. On full-size airplanes, this area ranges from a couple of inches (on a two-seater) to a couple of feet (for, say, a 747). On a paper airplane, this range is less than an inch long. If the balance point is forward of this region, the plane will dive at the ground. If it's behind this range, the plane will stall and tumble out of control. The best way to tell if your airplane is "pitch stable" is to give it a toss and see if it dives, swoops up

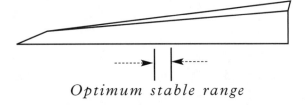

Optimum stable range

and down, or glides smoothly.

If you put a paper clip on the nose of your plane, it will become more stable. However, if you move the paper clip back, it will become less and less stable the farther you move it. Therefore, it would seem that to be on the safe side, you should put a lot of weight on the nose. Unfortunately, this doesn't work because if there is too much weight on the nose, the airplane will become overly stable and it will dive to the ground. (Lawn darts, for example, are extremely stable.)

Even if you have an airplane with pitch stability, your plane won't necessarily fly in a straight line. It also needs **DIRECTIONAL**

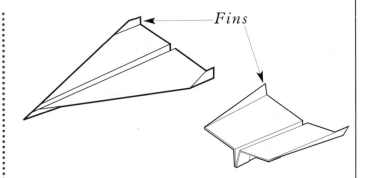

Fins

STABILITY, or it will spin around and fly backward. Having a fin on the back of the airplane will counteract its tendency to spin (just as the feathers on the back of arrows help them fly straight). On most paper airplanes, the body acts as the fin. If most of the plane's body is behind the balance point, it's a good bet it will be directionally stable. Bending the wingtips (fins) up or down will also contribute to the plane's directional stability.

The third type of stability is called **SPIRAL STABILITY.** If an airplane is spirally stable, it will fly in a straight line or a slow constant curve. A spirally unstable plane will begin to circle, turning tighter and tighter, until it spins down in a vertical dive. This is a very common problem, but it's easily corrected. When looking at the plane from the nose, bend the wings up slightly so they form a "Y" shape with the body, and make sure they are symmetrical.

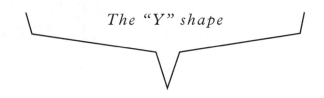

The "Y" shape

DRAG AND GLIDE ANGLE

When a glider flies, it must use gravity to overcome drag and keep it from slowing down, much like a bicycle coasting down a hill or a snow skier schussing down a mountain. By measuring the distance a glider flies, we can determine how much drag it has.

For this test, the higher your launching point, the better your results. Also it is important to use just a very gentle, slightly downward throw. Most gliders will fly the farthest if the back edge of the wing (called the elevator) is bent upward just a little bit. (If your glider veers, bend the rudder in the direction you want the plane to turn.)

MEASURE:

1) Launch height above ground (shoulder height above the floor)
2) Distance from launch point to where the plane first touches the floor
3) If possible, measure the weight of the glider. Most paper airplanes weigh from 4 to 8 grams; a standard sheet of paper weighs 4.5 grams

$$\text{Lift/Drag Ratio} = \frac{\text{(landing distance)}}{\text{(launch height)}}$$

$$\text{Drag} = \frac{\text{Weight}}{\text{(Lift/Drag Ratio)}}$$

COMPARISONS OF LIFT / DRAG RATIOS

Lift/Drag Ratio is a common measure of airplane efficiency.
The higher the number, the more efficient the airplane. Here are some comparisons:

REAL AIRPLANES

SPACE SHUTTLE	SMALL PROPELLER AIRPLANE	AIRLINER	SAILPLANE
			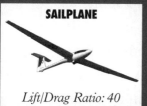
Lift/Drag Ratio: 4.7	*Lift/Drag Ratio: 10*	*Lift/Drag Ratio: 17*	*Lift/Drag Ratio: 40*

PAPER AIRPLANES

DART	SQUARE	EAGLE	WORLD RECORD AIRPLANE
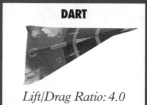			
Lift/Drag Ratio: 4.0	*Lift/Drag Ratio: 5.8*	*Lift/Drag Ratio: 5.8*	*Lift/Drag Ratio: 6.7*

Making Paper Airplanes

Fearless Folding

NOW THAT YOU UNDERSTAND the basic principles of flight, it's time to create a paper airplane. If you're just beginning your career as a paper airplane pilot, start with the dart or square models. They both fly well, and their simplicity allows you to spend less time folding and more time flying. Although it's not essential that all your creases lie exactly on the printed fold lines, they should fall near them. Fold along each line and then, on a hard flat surface, use your fingernail or the flat side of a pencil to make a sharp crease.

As you fold a plane, the paper will form an airfoil. The **AIRFOIL** is the shape of the wing when you look at your plane from the side. Thin flat airfoils work just fine on paper airplanes, although a little downward

Airflow

Airfoil

curvature near the front of the wing is helpful. Keep in mind, though, that paper airplanes do not need as much curvature as full-size airplanes, so don't overdo it.

If possible, keep the top of the wing smooth. The best place for the "pockets," or bulky folds that are formed when you make the plane, is on the bottom of the wing. Almost all of the planes in this book have the pockets on the bottom of the wings.

After folding the plane and setting the airfoil, hold it up and look at it from the front. Adjust the wings so that both wingtips are a little above the airplane body (the wings should form a slight "Y" shape with the body). Also, check to see if the wings are warped, and "unwarp" them

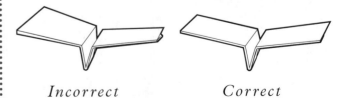

Incorrect   *Correct*

as necessary to get both wing angles the same. This is crucial to get the plane to perform as it should.

The Importance of Fine-Tuning

At this point, with your plane folded, the airfoil set, and any warp removed from the wings, there is less than a 50/50 chance of the plane flying well. Why? All airplanes need a little fine-tuning (some need a lot) to get them to fly properly.

Pitch (Elevator) Adjustments

Adjusting the pitch is the most important thing you can do to prevent your plane from diving or stalling. It's done by angling

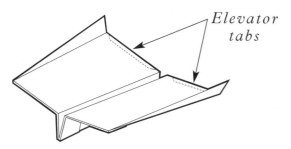

Elevator tabs

the **ELEVATOR,** which is a horizontal section of the plane, normally the back edge of the wing or tail. Bending the elevator up or down changes how nose high or nose low the airplane flies.

Throw the plane several times gently at a shallow downward angle, as described in "Best-Bet Throwing Techniques, Slow Flight," page 21. If the plane arcs down-

ward it may be properly adjusted for fast flight, but will need some "up elevator" for slow flight. Bend the elevator areas up a little bit (never bend them straight up or down). Most airplanes will need a little up elevator to fly properly for slow flight.

If the airplane climbs, slows, then dives, it has stalled and one of two things is wrong. You may have thrown the plane upward with too much speed. Make sure you are throwing gently and slightly downward. The second cause of stalling is too much up elevator. Fix this by bending the elevator down a little.

Continue fine-tuning the elevators until the airplane flies smoothly. If it refuses

ELEVATOR AND LIFT

How does elevator affect lift? Adding up elevator should result in the air pushing down on the tail of the plane, and, like a seesaw, raising the nose a little bit. Angling the nose up increases the lift. Prove this for yourself by measuring the flight distance and times as you progressively add more up elevator.

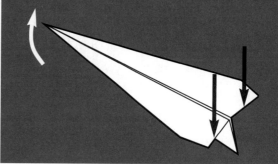

to do so, your plane may be tail heavy. Add some weight to the nose using a paper clip or a few pieces of tape, and repeat the pitch adjustment process.

If your plane has been adjusted to fly slowly and you want to fly it fast, bend the elevator down (otherwise it will stall when thrown hard). Planes adjusted to fly fast can be made to fly smoothly at a slow speed by adding up elevator.

Turning (Rudder) Adjustment

Most paper airplanes will have a tendency to veer to the left or right when they are first thrown. They can be adjusted using the

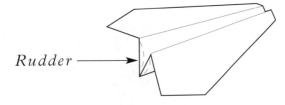

Rudder

back end or **RUDDER.** First, make sure the wingtips lie above the airplane body so the wings form a slight "Y" shape with the body.

This is important for the airplane to respond properly to the rudder. Throw the airplane gently downward at a shallow angle, making sure that you're not banking (tilting) the plane at all. If the airplane turns to the right, bend the rudder to the left. If the airplane turns to the left, bend the rudder to the right. Continue your test flights and rudder adjustments until the plane flies in a straight line. If the plane requires major rudder adjustments, one wing is probably warped. Check the wings again and adjust

them so they both look the same. If you want the airplane to veer right, bend the rudder a little to the right, and when you throw it, bank the airplane to the right (tilt the right wing slightly down). Reverse everything for a left turn.

Designing Your Own Paper Airplanes

The best way to begin designing your own airplanes is to modify the designs in this book. Try adding wingtip fins to an existing plane by bending the outermost half-inch of the wing up or down. Or make your plane's fuselage taller or narrower, longer or shorter. As you gain experience, you can create your own original designs by using the basic folding combinations shown in this book. Keep in mind that paper airplanes are seldom too nose heavy and they need strength up front where they impact floors, walls, and furniture. So most paper airplanes should have plenty of folded paper in the front of the wings or fuselage.

Other sections of this book, particularly "Why Paper Airplanes Crash," page 12,

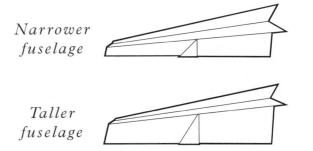

Narrower fuselage

Taller fuselage

and "The Importance of Fine-Tuning," page 17, are good background material, and will help you modify and adjust a new design so it flies properly.

When making your own paper airplanes, regular copier paper works well. Very light paper tends to be too flimsy, while very heavy paper is difficult to fold. Large sheets make big, but flimsy, paper airplanes. Very small sheets of paper produce small planes that are difficult to stabilize and fly smoothly. Your best bet is the common 8½-by-11-inch piece of paper.

Designing an original paper airplane

FIXING YOUR NEW DESIGN

PROBLEM AREA	SYMPTOM	FIX
PITCH STABILITY	Aircraft only dives or stalls even after repeated elevator adjustments	Add weight to the nose (e.g., a paper clip or tape). Add more wing area at the back of the airplane, less at the front.
DIRECTIONAL STABILITY	Aircraft rolls rapidly and dives	Make wingtip fins by bending the outer edges of the back of the wing up or down. Add a fin on the back of the plane (a temporary fin can be added by cutting a Post-it note). The front of the fuselage should be no taller than the fuselage at the back of the plane.
SPIRAL STABILITY	Aircraft rolls upside down (behaves similarly to directional stability, but slower)	Bend the wings up more (plane should look a little bit like the letter "Y" when viewed from the front or back). If the airplane has wingtip fins, make sure they are angled up instead of down.
WING STRENGTH	Wings bend upward too much in flight	Add more folds of paper where the wing meets the body, particularly at the front of the wing.

can be as simple or as detailed as you want it to be. The simplest new designs use a combination of diagonal and square folds, and more advanced designs may include cutting and taping sections together. Sometimes I begin a design with a particular look or configuration in mind. A replica of a real airplane is a good example of this. Sometimes I just begin folding without any idea of what I want to create, and see where the folds lead me. Sometimes a new design flies great, but many times it doesn't. If your plane doesn't fly well, begin with fine-tuning as described in "The Importance of Fine-Tuning" section. If that doesn't get your airplane flying, then more drastic steps may need to be taken, as described in the box on page 19.

Wingtips up and down

Replicas

Replicas may need a different construction technique than regular paper airplanes. Most real airplanes have longer and skinnier wings than paper airplanes. Paper is flimsy compared with the aluminum of actual airplanes, so paper airplane wings are usually short and stubby in order to make them stronger. As a result you should use a heavier paper, like a card stock or thin cardboard, when constructing replicas. Some real airplanes, like the Shuttle (included in this book) and jet fighters, already have short wings, so these are the best types of real planes to duplicate with regular paper.

Keep Your Chin Up!

Don't get discouraged if you have trouble getting your new design to work. I have seen many people who have a promising new design, but who give up on it too quickly to ever see it fly well. For every airplane we design for our books and calendars, at least two end up in the trash can. Perhaps the greatest tools for paper airplane making are patience and persistence.

Best-Bet Throwing Techniques

ONCE YOU'VE FOLDED AND fine-tuned a plane, the first thing you'll want to do is send it soaring. A good flight requires a good throw. The type of throw you use depends on the kind of flying you want to do and, to a lesser degree, on what plane you are using. The types of flying include slow flight, fast flight, and high (world record) throwing. All throws require a comfortable, secure grip on the plane, normally using the thumb and forefinger. Hold the plane on the bottom, near the front. The Chopper and Vortex use different throwing techniques which are covered in the folding and fine-tuning sections for those planes (pages 46 and 52, respectively).

SLOW FLIGHT is when a paper airplane glides slowly and steadily at a slight downward angle. I use this type of flying for fine-tuning my planes, for flying from buildings and hills, and for a lot of indoor flying. The launching technique for slow flight begins with holding the paper airplane in front of the shoulder. Push the airplane forward and slightly downward (most people want to

DEALING WITH A DUD

Every once in a while you will make a lemon. No matter how you try to adjust and fix it, the plane refuses to fly properly. The only way to really enjoy a dud is to wad it into a paper ball and go for two points in the trash can!

Almost all the

designs in this book are relatively simple and do not take much time to fold, so if a plane refuses to fly properly, you are better off just starting over. Don't get frustrated! Even though these planes are simple, when adjusted properly, they fly very well.

throw upward). Throw gently but firmly. The correct throwing speed will make a coin travel ten feet across the floor when thrown level from adult shoulder height (about six feet for a child).

FAST FLYING is when the plane flies fast and straight like an arrow. I use this type of flying for distance and accuracy competitions and for horsing around at home or the office. The best models for this are the Basic Dart and other similar-looking planes. Hold your plane in front of your shoulder for short throws (up to 15 feet), or above your shoulder for longer flights. Throw the plane gently and level for shorter distance, faster and a little upward for longer ones.

HIGH THROWING, the kind I used to break the world record, requires a powerful launch. Obviously, the World Record Paper Airplane is well suited for a hard throw,

but many other square designs can be thrown this way as well.

The airplane will go up a long way, so you will need a high ceiling if you are not outdoors. Adjust the airplane so that a gentle toss results in a smooth, slowly turning flight. Then, throw the airplane as hard as you can straight up. If it flies properly, it will spiral up, level off, and glide slowly in a large gentle turn.

Don't get discouraged if you don't set a record with your first throw. Only about one out of every five paper airplanes I make really climbs well. You will most likely have to make several planes before you get one that you are satisfied with. Remember to adjust the plane to glide well with just a gentle throw before trying for the record. And don't forget to try small adjustments to the elevator and rudder to improve the climb and glide.

Ken Blackburn demonstrating his world record throw

WHAT MAKES A PAPER AIRPLANE FLY THE FARTHEST?

Flight distance is affected by different things, including how the paper airplane is thrown. Hard throws result in fast flight, and your best bet for a long flight is a small-winged plane (such as a dart) so it can fly through the air like a javelin. If the plane is thrown gently, it glides at slow speed and big wings are best.

FAST LAUNCH

☞ Generally produces the longest flights on level ground.

☞ Wings produce little lift, and should be as small as practical to minimize drag.

☞ Flights up to 200 feet possible (though most flights are no more than 50 feet).

☞ Long pointy planes are best. Length helps to keep them flying straight, and pointy small wings minimize drag.

SLOW LAUNCH

☞ Generally produces the longest flights from an elevation.

☞ At slow speeds wings produce a lot of lift. The wings should be as large as practical to minimize drag and therefore maximize distance.

☞ Square planes are best for long-lasting flights. Wide, straight wings produce the least drag at low speeds, which is why birds and sailplanes use them.

☞ Bend back edge of wing up a little bit to enable slow flight.

☞ Depending on the style of plane, in calm air glide distance will equal between three and six times launch height. See illustration below.

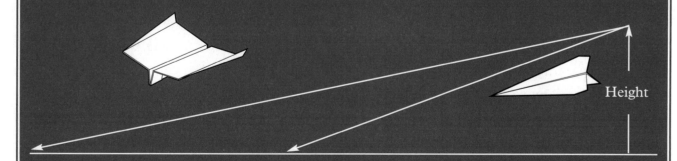

Height

Square plane distance = 5 x height   Pointy plane distance = 3 x height

Optimal Airfields

ONE OF THE BEAUTIES OF PAPER airplanes is that you can make them quickly and fly them anywhere. Indoors, they can play the role of carrier pigeon conveying a message to a nearby friend or colleague, repurpose a boring or irritating memo, or simply while away a few spare minutes. Outdoors, they can catch a rising air current and soar like a bird or, with the wind behind them, fly hundreds of feet before landing. What follows is a look at how to make the best flights in whatever environment you find yourself.

Flying at Home or in the Office

Don't be discouraged by the size of your home or office. Any room at least ten feet long is a potential flying field. And while you need at least 50 to 60 feet of ceiling height to set a world record, there's a lot of fun flying to be had in rooms with eight-foot ceilings. Instead of keeping the plane aloft for many seconds or getting it to fly a

great distance, the challenge becomes making accurate throws and performing stunts in a restricted space. So rather than looking at walls, tables, and ceilings as obstacles and barriers, consider them challenges waiting to be met.

The following are some things I have tried over the years to increase the enjoyment of indoor flying:

☞ Flying airplanes back and forth with a friend
☞ Landing on a target
☞ Performing stunts (see "The Art of Aerobatics," page 29)

The Plane Game

This is a modified game of catch. The challenge for the thrower is to get the plane close enough to the catcher so he or she can reach it. Meanwhile, the catcher's challenge is to pluck the plane from the air without bending or crushing it. Once you are able to throw the airplane accurately, try some variations with your throws. For example, aim your throw to the left of your partner, but throw the plane with the wings tilted to the right. (This will cause the airplane to turn, or bank, right.) If you are left-handed, point the plane to the right and bank left. Once you get the hang of it you will be able to throw a paper airplane to your partner along a curved path.

The more you tilt the wings, the more bank you will have. Try **BANKING** the plane more for a more curved flight path, or less for a straighter path. Once you've mastered the art of banking, you can fly your plane around furniture or even a wall.

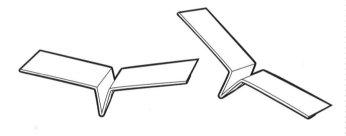

Level   *Banked*

Another variation involves throwing your plane high or low. Throw the airplane at a gentle downward angle with more speed. If the plane is properly trimmed, it will start to fly toward the ground and then swoop back up so that your partner can catch it. You can also try throwing your plane gently upward. This should cause the plane to climb a little, slow down, and then nose over and glide downward to your partner. Once you get the hang of swooping the plane up or down, try banking its wings, and you will achieve dives or climbs along a curved flight path. (Hint: For steep-banked

turns, try adding some up elevator to your airplane by bending up the back edge of the wing a little more.)

Perfect Landings

This exercise tests a different kind of accuracy. Place the runway from this book (airstrip side up) on a spot on the floor across the room, and try to land your airplane on it. See if you can make the plane stop as close as possible to the end of the strip. When this starts getting easier, stand farther back. Imagine that you have passengers and go for as smooth a landing as possible. Or turn the runway over and aim for the bull's-eye. Throw the plane ten times, tallying your score as you go.

You can also use a piece of furniture as a landing zone. For example, it does not take too much imagination to picture a table as an aircraft carrier. (I guess I'll never truly grow up.) This image can make it all the more rewarding when you make a perfect landing—and very disappointing when the plane skims the table and slides off the end or misses completely and crashes to the ground. Try spot landings with several types of airplanes. I find dart-style planes best for this activity.

When I practice spot landings, I usually choose two different targets (for example, the runway and a table) at opposite ends of a room. I make two or three planes and try for the first target. Then I go across the room, pick up the planes, and aim for the second target. Inevitably, someone comes along, and usually boredom or a competitive spirit will draw my new flight-training buddy into a spot-landing contest with me.

Flying Outdoors

I really enjoy the freedom of flying paper airplanes outside, where there are no walls or ceilings to block your flight. (You would, however, be amazed at the number of paper-airplane–hungry trees there are in this world. You may want to bring extra planes and/or paper with you.) On calm days, you can fly with a friend, land on a target, or perform aerobatics just as you would indoors. However, outdoor flying also provides an opportunity that is unavailable with indoor flying/soaring. On many occasions, I have watched my paper airplane as it climbed higher and higher in the sky; every once in a while, it has even soared up and out of sight.

AIR CURRENTS are what allow a glider to maintain or gain altitude. Full-size gliders have flown over 1,000 miles using wind currents, and I've used wind currents while hang gliding to gain about half a mile in altitude and to stay aloft for over three hours. Paper airplanes can use the wind just like full-size gliders. The trick is to figure out where the rising air currents are and to fly your paper airplane into them.

Why rising air? A well-trimmed paper airplane descends through the air at about three or four feet per second. If the air rises at the same rate as the paper airplane descends,

the plane will stay at the same altitude. If the air is rising more than three or four feet per second, the plane flies upward. It is fairly common to find areas where air is rising at ten to 20 feet per second, which will cause your paper airplane to zoom skyward. There are two basic reasons why air rises: ridge lift and convection (aka thermals).

Ridge Lift

When wind hits a telephone pole, it goes around the pole. But when wind collides with a large hill or building, the majority of air goes up and over it. This rising air in front of buildings or hills, called **RIDGE LIFT,** is the air you are looking for to carry your paper airplane upward. It is important that the hill or building face almost directly into the wind. If it does not, the wind will simply be pushed to the side instead of upward and your airplane will not soar.

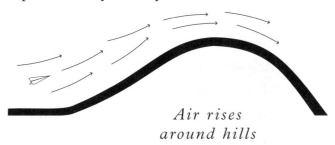

*Air rises
around hills*

How high up can a paper airplane go while soaring in ridge lift? A general rule of thumb is that in moderate wind a glider can rise about twice the height of the hill. So on a ten-foot hill, your plane could rise to 20 feet. Similarly, on a 1,000-foot mountain your paper airplane could soar up to 2,000 feet!

In comparison, a lot of wind normally

passes around rather than over buildings, so do not expect to double your paper airplane's altitude over a building. Nonetheless, the wind rising in front of the building certainly can give your plane a boost. I like to launch planes in front of a building, on the side facing the wind, at a distance of about half the height of the building. The plane will circle and drift toward the building, often climbing in the rising air in front of it.

Catching rising air around buildings can be tricky

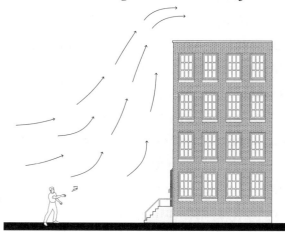

You can also launch paper airplanes through the windows on the windward side of buildings. If all goes well, the plane catches the rising air and starts climbing. Often, however, the wind crashes the plane into the side of the building. So I actually prefer launching paper airplanes from the side of the building facing away from the wind. Although you do not get the ridge lift of the windward side, your plane will fly for a long way, and may even begin to climb due to thermals it encounters en route.

Hills are perhaps the best flying fields.

Standing on the hill, adjust the plane so it flies straight, then very gently release it into the wind and watch it hover or slowly climb in front of you. On larger hills, use the Basic Square Plane or World Record Airplane and throw it upward (using the world record launch) to get it away from the hill and up into the rising air currents.

Mountains can also be an exciting place to fly paper airplanes. The air currents go upward for hundreds or thousands of feet. The biggest problem with mountains is getting the paper airplane away from the obstacles—such as trees, buildings, or even people—near the launch site. Try using a pointed airplane, adjusted for straight flight, and launching it from the side of the mountain facing into the wind. If the wind is right and the plane is adjusted well, it could fly up and out of sight.

You can also use a Basic Square Plane, launching it upward to initially get it away from the mountain. As with buildings, it is also fun to launch paper airplanes from the side of the mountain facing downwind. The paper airplane may not rise, but it sure will fly a very long distance.

Convection or Thermals

The second type of rising air comes from thermals, or areas of warm, rising air. The sun heats up some areas of the ground more than others, and as we all know, hot air rises. Sometimes it rises in bubbles, sometimes in a continuous column, and as it does so, it drifts with the wind.

Dry sunny places are good thermal generators. And the darker the ground is, the hotter it will become, and the larger the thermal. For example, asphalt parking lots often generate big thermals. (Cool places, like lakes, oceans, or forests, make the air sink, instead of rise. Think of this effect as an "anti-thermal.")

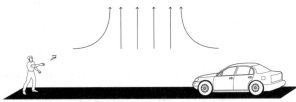

Blacktop generates thermals

The best way to use **THERMALS** for soaring paper airplanes is to go to the downwind edge of a thermal-generating area. The rising hot air from the area up-wind will be passing over you. Use a good Basic Square Plane or World Record Air-plane and adjust it to fly in circles about 20 or 30 feet wide. Throw the plane as high as possible, and do not get frustrated if it does not climb up and out of sight on your first few throws. Thermals are not well organized close to the ground, and they do not rise continuously, making them tricky to catch.

Be ready to launch your plane as soon as the wind picks up or shifts. As a thermal develops, air near the ground is sucked from all directions into its bottom. So if you notice a sudden wind shift, it is likely an indicator that there is a thermal somewhere

in the direction that the wind is getting sucked. Throw your plane in that direction.

Flying in Large Indoor Areas

I personally love large indoor areas. This may be obvious since I needed a large space each time I set the world record. The most accessible big areas I've found are school gymnasiums and auditoriums—they're large enough for aerobatics and most time-aloft flying. Contact the person in charge of the space, explain what you'd like to use it for, and he or she will likely let you use it when it is free.

For serious, world-record-class time aloft, however, you need at least 50 feet of ceiling space. Unfortunately, this is hard to come by at local high schools. Better bets are college gymnasiums, college basketball stadiums (where I set my first world record), city coliseums, and city convention centers (where I set my second world record).

I'm continually trying new adjustments to my paper airplanes, and large indoor areas are great for testing them out. Outdoors, wind gusts result in inconsistent flight times, but the controlled environment of an indoor space allows me to accurately check flight times and determine whether a modification really helps. Large indoor areas are also ideal for holding paper air-plane contests (see page 32).

The Art of Aerobatics

PERFORMING AEROBATICS (STUNTS) requires a mastery of adjusting and throwing. Once you achieve this, you'll find it very satisfying to watch your plane do just what you want —be it a circle, loop, dive, or tailslide. But probably the most rewarding aspect of aerobatics is the impression you'll make on your coworkers when you casually perform stunts in the office.

For spot landings and back-and-forth throwing just about any type of paper airplane will do, but for stunts the best planes to use are the Stunt Plane, Basic Square Plane, or World Record Airplane. Before trying to perform aerobatics with any plane, adjust it so it flies in a straight line. It'll also probably help to add some up elevator. As you remember, up elevator requires you to bend the back edge of the wing up a little. This extra up elevator will probably make the nose bob-

ble up and down when the plane is flown gently, but it will help the plane turn during aerobatics.

Circles

A **CIRCLE** is when the airplane follows a circular path around the room so that you can catch it without taking a step. For right-handers, a circle is most easily done by banking the plane's wings to the right and throwing it with a little extra speed. You may need to give the plane a little right rudder to keep it circling and to prevent it from leveling its wings and flying straight. Left-handers should add some left rudder trim, and throw the airplane with the wings banked left. You'll notice that if you bank the wings too much or throw too softly, the plane will start to circle, then fly downward to the ground. If you bank the wings too little or throw too hard the plane will circle, but

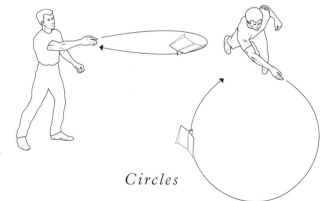

Circles

it will also climb and probably stall. When the plane is properly adjusted and you get your throwing technique polished, you can stand still and perform circle after circle. My record is 20 circles in a row. I've also tried to make an airplane do two continuous circles before catching it, but I haven't quite accomplished that—yet.

Loops

A **LOOP** is when the airplane flies in a vertical circle. This maneuver is easiest to achieve outside or in a large space like a gym, but it is possible to do a loop in a standard-size room, where the low ceiling makes it just a little more challenging.

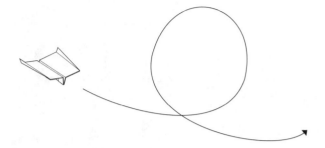

Throw slightly downward

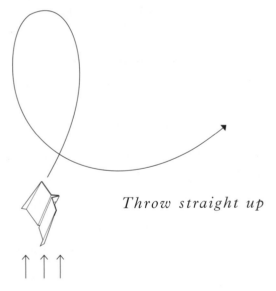

Throw straight up

First, make sure the wings are even and the airplane has a lot of up elevator—the back edge of the wing should be bent about halfway between lying flat and straight up. The easiest way to make a paper airplane loop is to hold it with wings level (i.e., not banked in either direction) and the nose pointed straight up, and give it a gentle throw. The plane should climb to near the ceiling, then fall over on its back, and finally pull out to level flight before hitting the floor. Be patient. It will take a few throws to get the correct upward angle and the correct throwing velocity.

The next way to get a paper airplane to loop is a little more difficult as well as a little more exciting. Try throwing the plane slightly downward with a strong throw. The airplane should pull up before hitting the floor, climb upward, fall over backward just short of the ceiling, and then pull out from the resulting dive. Once again, it will

VARIATION ON A THEME

Try banking your plane's wings just a little. Then throw the plane exactly like you would for a vertical loop. Instead of the airplane performing a straight up and down loop, the plane will fly an angled loop.

probably take a few throws to achieve the proper dive angle on the throw as well as the correct throwing speed.

Note: I have found that some airplanes are duds, and no matter what you do, they just simply will not be able to perform loops very well. If this happens, you're probably best off making a new plane or using a different design.

Dives and Tailslides

A **DIVE** is when an airplane is flying directly at the ground. A tailslide is sort of a backward dive—the plane's nose is pointed straight up, but the plane is flying backward toward the ground. Paper airplanes are amazing because not only can they start in a dive or tailslide then correct themselves before crashing to the floor, but they can accomplish this with only about six or seven feet of altitude, in approximately one second.

To perform a dive, start by adding extra up elevator on your plane. Hold the airplane as high as you can above your head and a little bit in front of you. If you are not very tall, stand on a stool or chair. Point the nose straight down and drop the plane. It should

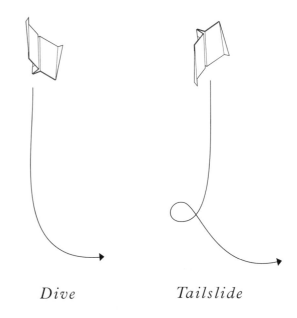

Dive   *Tailslide*

pull out of the dive in a very short time.

To watch your airplane pull itself out of a **TAILSLIDE,** hold it as you would for a dive (high above your head and a little bit in front of you). This time, point the nose upward and then drop the plane. The airplane will start into a tailslide, but quickly flip over into a dive, and then pull out. As a matter of fact, you should be able to hold the plane with the nose up at any angle and with wings banked left or right, and the plane should be capable of pulling itself out of the maneuver and flying straight. The reason the plane "knows" which way to fly is because it is stable. Their stability is what differentiates paper airplanes from tumbling pieces of paper.

Competitive Flying

EVER SINCE THE SECOND PAPER airplane was folded, there have been paper airplane contests. The beauty of them is that they can be organized quickly, participated in by all, and can take many different forms. The following are some considerations for organizing a contest, as well as some tips for taking home the trophy.

Organizing a Contest

I have attended many contests in my time, and have been amazed at the tremendous variety among them. Some take place indoors; others are outdoors. Some require participants to launch from the ground; others provide an elevated platform. Some regulate how the planes are made; in others anything goes. Often, the parameters of the contest are determined by what locations are available, the number of volunteers on hand to help organize and judge the events, the number of entrants, and of course the personal preferences of the organizer.

Location

The first decision you'll likely make is where to hold the contest. The easiest location is the great **OUTDOORS,** specifically your own backyard or, better, a local park or school athletic field. The advantages of outdoor contests are ready availability, a lack of obstructions, and the potential for some very long duration and distance flights. The major disadvantages are the possibility of bad weather and the potential for disorganization. For example, at one contest I attended the wind was blowing, which resulted in several flights over 100 feet. However, they were all in different directions, making them hard to measure and giving the contest a chaotic feel.

Outdoor contests are probably most appropriate for small groups. The smaller the group, the easier it is to reschedule a contest canceled due to bad weather. Likewise, if the weather is excellent, it's easier to organize a spontaneous contest with a smaller group.

INDOOR CONTESTS are normally

preferred because they provide a controlled environment for the events and can take place regardless of the weather. A large space (approximately 20 feet high, 40 feet wide, and 80 feet long), such as a school basketball court, will do fine. However, if you are planning on a large contest with numerous events and participants, try to find a bigger space, such as the gymnasium at a college, community center, or large high school. Although city coliseums and convention centers are great places for paper airplane contests, they can be very expensive and are not easily reserved.

Beware of indoor air currents

Wherever you hold your indoor contest, it must be well lighted and obstructions, such as basketball baskets and seats, should be removed or retracted as much as possible. The judges' table should be in a prominent spot where contestants can register, find out about different events, and learn the results of the contests.

Keep in mind that open doors and windows as well as ventilation systems can create wild currents indoors. If it is practical, shut all doors and windows and turn off the ventilation system during the contests. Otherwise contestants may complain that the winner of an event had an unfair advantage due to a sudden wind current.

Event Categories

The most common events include maximum time aloft, maximum distance, accuracy, and replication of a famous aircraft.

You can also have events based on the construction of the aircraft, with some events for planes made with several sheets of paper, tape, glue and/or ballast, and others for airplanes constructed from one sheet of paper supplied immediately before the event. Although I have rarely seen it, I think it would be a good idea to supply paper with folding instructions, which would result in a "one design" contest in which everyone flies the same type of airplane.

As the size of a contest grows, contestants may need to be divided into **CATEGORIES** for better organization. This will also provide more people a better opportunity to win. Age groups are one natural category, especially since younger children are not as strong as older children or adults, and cannot throw paper airplanes as far or as high. Each group should have a minimum of three contestants, but not more than twenty.

Another organizational basis is skill level. For example, people who work with aircraft for a living or have hobbies involving real or model aircraft can be categorized as "professionals." Those who have no such backgrounds are "amateurs." Contest organizers can determine their own criteria for professional vs. amateur based on the types of people in the contests. One long running, annual paper airplane contest I have attended defines a professional as one who has previously won an event and an amateur as someone who has not.

Construction

There are no official rules anywhere that define what a paper airplane is or can be. As a result, each contest or event needs rules specifying the type and weight of paper, number of sheets, and the modifications that can be made with scissors, glue, tape, paper clips, et cetera, allowed.

Some contests allow paper airplanes to be made of any sheet-like paper product, including poster board, which can be cut and glued together to create a balsa-wood–like, hand-launched glider. Clearly such a plane would have an advantage over one made from much flimsier stock, so it helps to have rules governing paper weight. Usually, contests do not need to worry about placing a limit on the minimum thickness of paper, as very thin paper, such as tracing paper, is too flimsy to make a paper airplane capable of winning an event.

For events that require launching paper airplanes from the floor, the size of the airplane makes little difference and no rules are needed curtailing size. But for a time-aloft event that has a platform launch site, larger airplanes can have an advantage. A rule limiting the amount of paper may be necessary to keep the airplanes to a reasonable size. It is also important for platform time-aloft events to have a rule for minimum airplane size. At one contest in Georgia, a contestant ripped off a tiny corner of a piece of paper and let it slowly flutter to the ground—and won the contest! This can be avoided by requiring a minimum amount of paper, a minimum wingspan, or a steady, non-tumbling flight for all airplanes entered in the event.

Most paper airplanes can be improved by cutting, gluing, and/or taping, and most contests allow these activities to some degree. (Replica events usually allow tape, glue, and cutting so that realistic-looking planes can be made.) The problem with glue and even tape is that the planes become much more elaborate. It takes more time to build them and decreases the amount of competition in the events because only very experienced people will be able to enter. Normally, if a contest has a time-aloft or distance event allowing tape or glue, there will be another similar event with more restrictive requirements, opening up the competition to everyone interested.

BALLAST is weight added to the nose or tail of an airplane to help it fly better. Occasionally, I add a couple of layers of tape to the nose of a pointed paper airplane

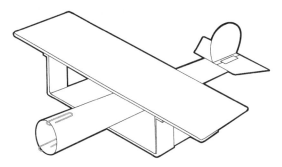

Ballast can add stability

to improve flying. Distance events may need a ballast limit, such as one paper clip per airplane, to prevent contestants from building paper lawn darts. Most time-aloft paper airplanes are hurt by large amounts of ballast, so generally no rules are needed regarding ballast for these events.

Rules for Throwing

Each event needs rules for throwing the paper airplanes. For example, who will throw the airplane, the contestant or judge? How many airplanes is each contestant allowed? How many throws are allowed for each airplane?

In most contests, the contestants throw their own airplanes, and the limit is one or two airplanes per person per event. The number of throws is usually limited in one of two ways: by allotting a specified number of throws per airplane or a time limit for throwing. Many contests allow each contestant three throws. Alternatively, contestants are allowed as many throws as they can achieve in a certain time, usually two or three minutes. And sometimes there is

a time limit for each event as a whole, say 15 to 30 minutes. Contestants form a line, and the first person makes a throw. After the judges have recorded the time or distance of the flight, the contestant retrieves the paper airplane and goes to the end of the line. Then the next contestant throws. The cycle is repeated until time expires, with each contestant making several launches. This time limit keeps the entire contest on schedule, no matter how many contestants enter. In all of the above formats, the best flight during the period is used for judging.

Taking Home the Trophy

Creating a champion paper airplane takes skill, patience, and a little bit of luck. The airplanes in this book are ideal for winning most contests.

Time-aloft events launched from the ground are best performed by—surprise, surprise—the World Record Airplane. It should always be thrown using the world record throwing technique as described on page 22. However, for time-aloft events starting from a platform, the Falcon is a better choice. Its descent rate is a little slower than that of the World Record Airplane.

For distance and accuracy events, the Eagle or Interceptor are your best bets. Fly both and choose the one you are the most comfortable with. If the contest allows it, add extra weight (such as a paper clip or tape) to the nose. For outdoor distance contests, use the World Record Airplane. Throw it as high as possible, letting the wind take it on a long flight.

As I mentioned in the introduction, your throw is almost as important as your plane. For time aloft, condition your arm well in advance of the event. For accuracy and aerobatics, nothing beats practice, practice, and more practice.

PAPER AIRPLANE CONTEST FOR TEAMS

Most paper airplane contests are for individuals, but sometimes it's fun to make it a team event. Here is a sample set of rules for a team accuracy event.

CONSTRUCTION

☞ One sheet of 8½-by-11-inch copier paper (20 or 24 pound paper) is permitted for each plane.

☞ Plane must be paper only—no tape, glue, paper clips, or any other material may be used.

☞ Plane must have aerodynamic surfaces (no paper balls allowed!).

☞ Pilot's name and team must be written on each plane.

CONTEST

☞ Each team will be announced, and given time to assemble at the throwing line. Each team will be given 2 minutes to fly its planes.

☞ Points are awarded based on where the planes finish on a series of concentric rings marked on the floor in the flight area. When time is over, all planes must remain stationary until judges determine scoring.

☞ Points are awarded for the highest scoring area any part of the plane touches, including the boundary markings.

☞ Planes may deflect off walls, ceiling, or furniture.

☞ Bull's-eye scores 10 points, small circle 3 points, outer circle 1 point.

☞ Each person can rethrow their plane as many times within the 2 minutes as desired. Teammates can help recover planes.

Folding and Fine-Tuning Instructions

General Guidelines

THE UPCOMING PLANES ARE all marked with dashed and dotted lines. These are your folding guides. Try to make your creases as sharp as possible.

There is an essential difference between the dashed and dotted lines: The **DASHED** lines are what we call "fold-in" lines. This means that these lines will be on the inside of a crease and you will not be able to see them once the plane is folded up. These are the ones that are numbered.

The **DOTTED** lines are "fold-away" lines. They'll be visible after the fold is completed. The dotted lines are simply guides on the reverse side of the dashed lines to help ensure that you're folding in the right place.

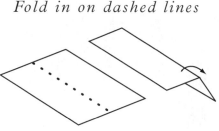

Fold in on dashed lines

Fold away on dotted lines

A few of the planes require you to use scissors, and on these you'll see thick **SOLID** cut lines. The cut lines are indicated with scissor icons as well.

The fold marks are in numerical order. Once you get familiar with the technique, you'll likely be able to fold many of the planes without referring to the schematic folding instructions on the following pages.

Do your best to make your folds along the dashed and dotted lines, but don't worry if you can't exactly match them. In fact, in some cases, owing to shifts in printing, it'll be almost impossible to do so. Just try to stick as close to them as you can. Do make sure, however, that your plane's wings are even. If they end up being different shapes or sizes, it'll be hard to get the plane to fly well.

THE BASIC SQUARE PLANE

THIS PLANE IS VERY SIMPLE, BUT it's good for stunts and long-lasting flights. In fact, the World Record Airplane is based on it. It's an excellent airplane to begin experimenting with because it's easily modified. This version doesn't have fins, but you can add them for extra stability.

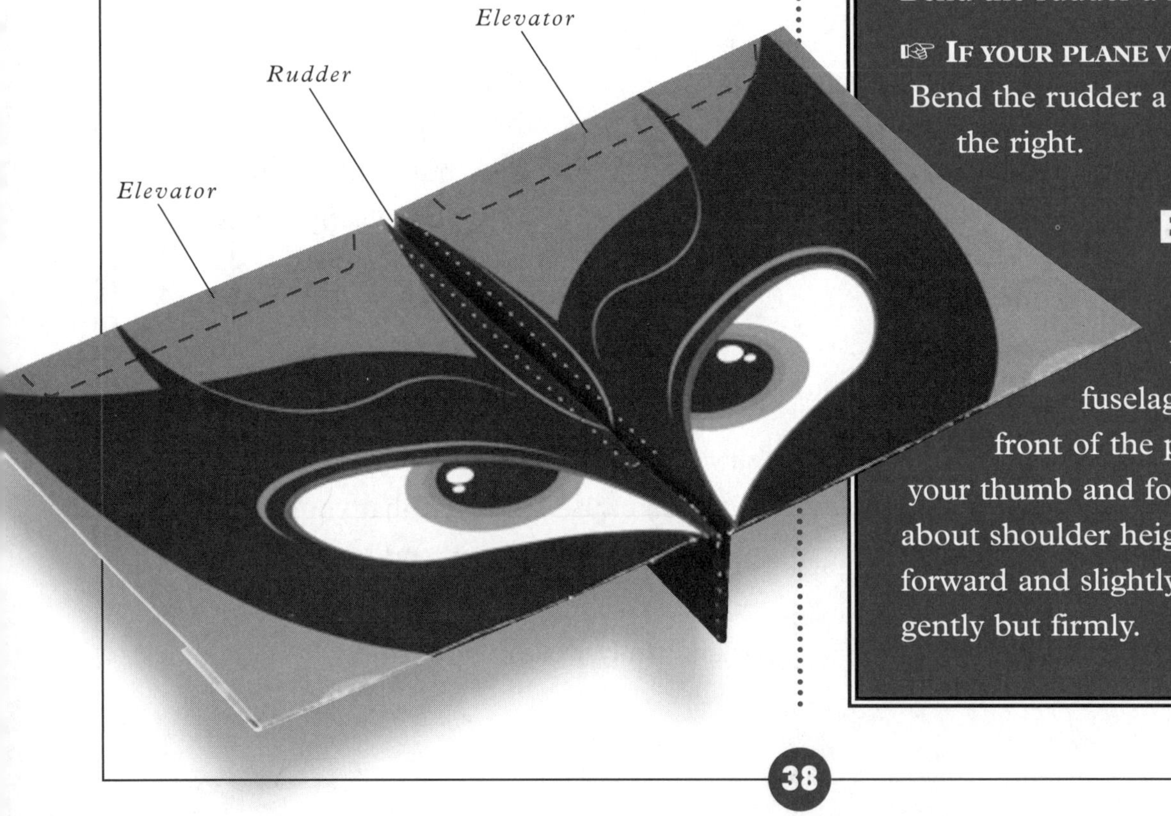

Elevator

Rudder

Elevator

FLIGHT ADJUSTMENTS

☞ **IF YOUR PLANE DIVES:** Bend the elevators up a little *or* throw the plane a little faster.

☞ **IF YOUR PLANE CLIMBS, SLOWS, THEN DIVES:** Bend the elevators down a little *or* throw the plane a little slower.

☞ **IF YOUR PLANE VEERS RIGHT:** Bend the rudder a little to the left.

☞ **IF YOUR PLANE VEERS LEFT:** Bend the rudder a little to the right.

BEST-BET THROW

Hold the fuselage toward the front of the plane between your thumb and forefinger at about shoulder height. Push plane forward and slightly downward gently but firmly.

Remember: Fold in on dashed lines; fold away on dotted lines.

1. Start with flames side up. Fold along line 1 to line 2.

2. Fold along line 2 to line 3, and line 3 to line 4.

3. Fold along lines 4 to 8.

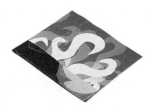

4. Flip plane over and fold in half along centerline, fold 9.

5. Fold one wing up along line 10.

6. Flip plane over. Fold wing down along line 11.

Bend elevators up slightly for best flight.

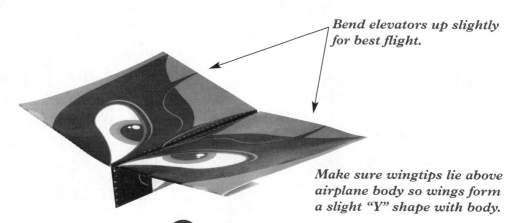

Make sure wingtips lie above airplane body so wings form a slight "Y" shape with body.

THE BASIC DART

THIS IS PROBABLY THE MOST common type of paper airplane. It's simple, quick to fold, and flies fast and far. You've likely seen or even tried many variations of this model. Wingtip fins and up elevator are important to maintain level flight. You may also want to add a couple of pieces of tape or a paper clip to the nose for extra stability.

Elevator

Rudder

Elevator

FLIGHT ADJUSTMENTS

☞ **IF YOUR PLANE DIVES:** Bend the elevators up a little *or* throw the plane a little faster.

☞ **IF YOUR PLANE CLIMBS, SLOWS, THEN DIVES:** Bend the elevators down a little *or* throw the plane a little slower.

☞ **IF YOUR PLANE VEERS RIGHT:** Bend the rudder a little to the left.

☞ **IF YOUR PLANE VEERS LEFT:** Bend the rudder a little to the right.

BEST-BET THROW

Hold the fuselage toward the front of the plane between your thumb and forefinger. For shorter flights, hold the plane in front of your shoulder and give it a gentle, level push forward. For longer flights, hold the plane above your shoulder and throw it faster and a little upward.

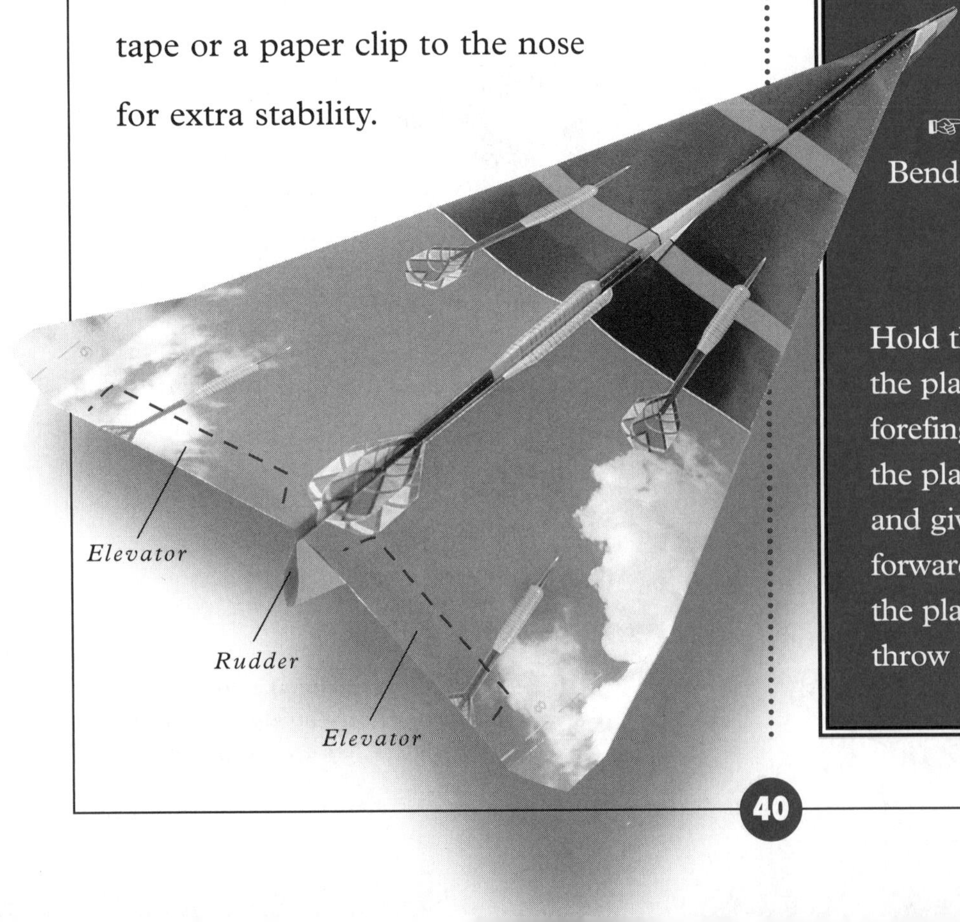

Remember: Fold in on dashed lines; fold away on dotted lines.

1. Crease along centerline, fold 5, and reopen.

2. Flip plane over and fold along lines 1 and 2.

3. Fold along lines 3 and 4.

4. Flip plane over and fold down along centerline, line 5.

5. Fold one wing up along line 6.

6. Flip plane over, and fold wing down along line 7.

7. Fold wingtips up along lines 8 and 9.

Bend elevators up slightly for best flight.

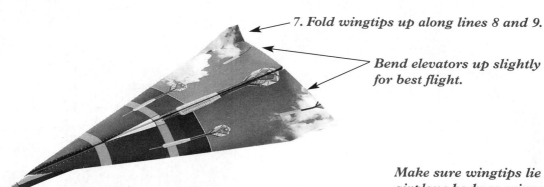

Make sure wingtips lie above airplane body so wings form a slight "Y" shape with body.

THE STUNT PLANE

THE STUNT PLANE PERFORMS aerobatics well because of its tail design. When you cut away the paper as shown, the tail becomes very easy to adjust, making the plane good for loops and turns. In addition, when it's thrown high, it stays aloft very well.

Rudder
Elevators

FLIGHT ADJUSTMENTS

☞ **IF YOUR PLANE DIVES:** Bend the elevators up a little *or* throw the plane a little faster.

☞ **IF YOUR PLANE CLIMBS, SLOWS, THEN DIVES:** Bend the elevators down a little *or* throw the plane a little slower.

☞ **IF YOUR PLANE VEERS RIGHT:** Bend the rudder a little to the left.

☞ **IF YOUR PLANE VEERS LEFT:** Bend the rudder a little to the right.

BEST-BET THROW

For everyday flying, hold the fuselage toward the front of the plane between your thumb and forefinger at about shoulder height. Push plane foward and slightly downward gently but firmly. For stunt flying, see page 29. For high throws, see page 22.

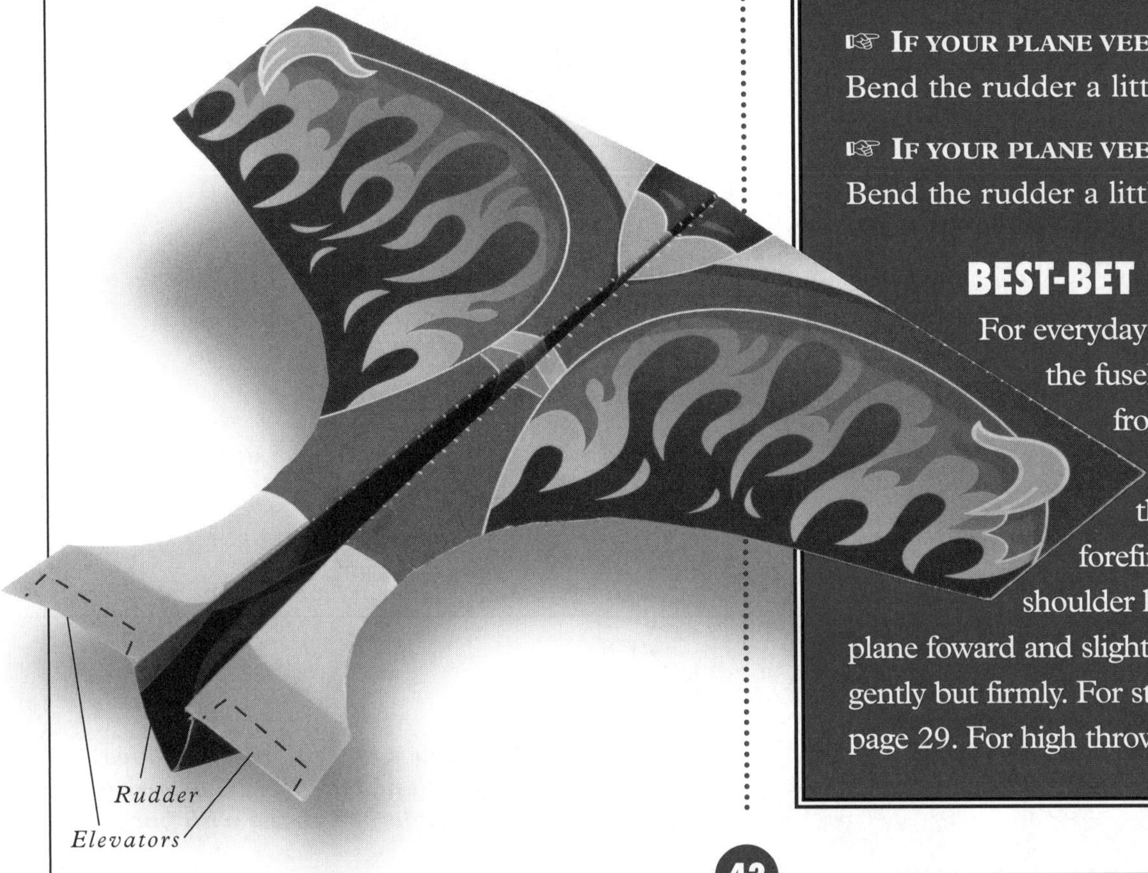

Remember: Cut on solid green lines; fold in on dashed lines; fold away on dotted lines.

Cut here

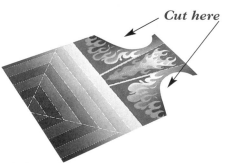

1. Cut along solid green lines as shown.

2. Fold along lines 1 and 2.

3. Fold nose up along line 3 to line 4, and along line 4 to line 5.

4. Fold on lines 5 through 9.

5. Flip plane over and fold in half along centerline, fold 10.

6. Fold one wing up along line 11.

7. Flip plane over and fold other wing down along line 12.

Bend elevators up slightly for best flight.

Make sure wingtips lie above airplane body so wings form a slight "Y" shape with body.

THE EAGLE

THE EAGLE IS A VERY STABLE glider. It's a type of dart, but this design has more paper in the nose than most darts, giving it extra stability. The Eagle is a good long-distance, precision flier, but it generally needs a little up elevator to achieve its best glide path. Try experimenting with different fin types and see how they affect the flight.

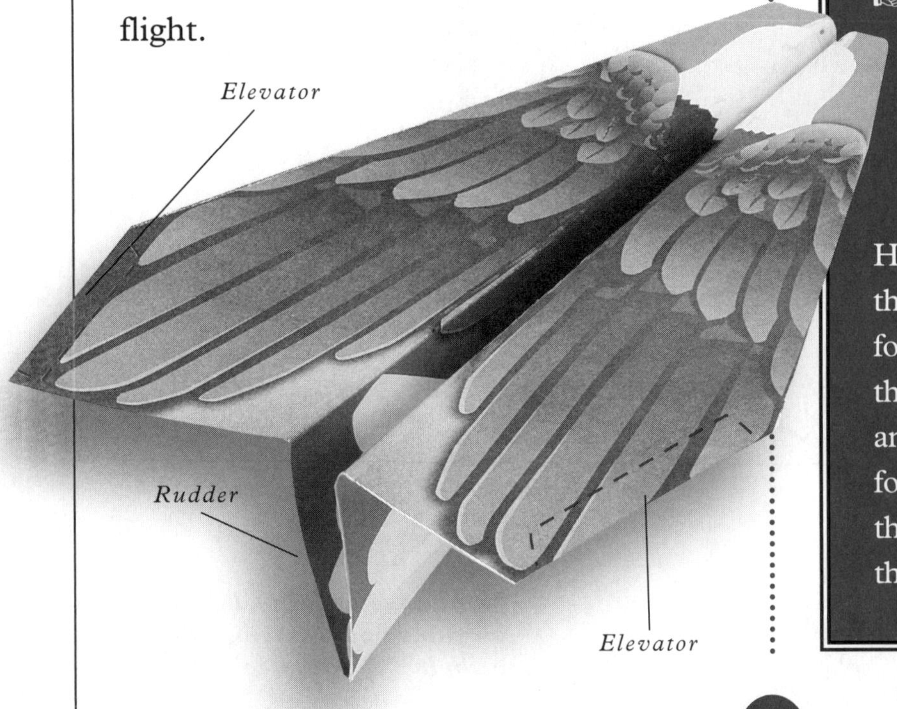

Elevator

Rudder

Elevator

FLIGHT ADJUSTMENTS

☞ **IF YOUR PLANE DIVES:** Bend the elevators up a little *or* throw the plane a little faster.

☞ **IF YOUR PLANE CLIMBS, SLOWS, THEN DIVES:** Bend the elevators down a little *or* throw the plane a little slower.

☞ **IF YOUR PLANE VEERS RIGHT:** Bend the rudder a little to the left.

☞ **IF YOUR PLANE VEERS LEFT:** Bend the rudder a little to the right.

BEST-BET THROW

Hold the fuselage toward the front of the plane between your thumb and forefinger. For shorter flights, hold the plane in front of your shoulder and give it a gentle, level push forward. For longer flights, hold the plane above your shoulder and throw it faster and a little upward.

Remember: Fold in on dashed lines; fold away on dotted lines.

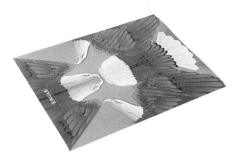

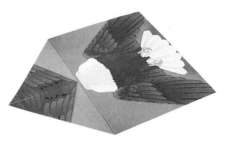

1. Crease along centerline, fold 7, and reopen.

2. Flip plane over and fold along lines 1 and 2.

3. Fold along line 3.

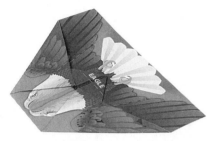

4. Fold flaps in on lines 4 and 5.

5. Fold point down on line 6.

6. Flip plane over and fold in half along its centerline, fold 7.

7. Fold one wing down along line 8.

8. Flip plane over and fold other wing down along line 9.

Bend elevators up slightly for best flight.

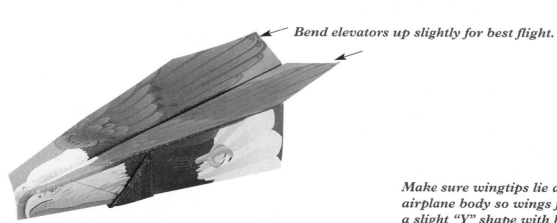

Make sure wingtips lie above airplane body so wings form a slight "Y" shape with body.

THE CHOPPER

ALTHOUGH THIS ISN'T REALLY AN airplane, the Chopper is a fun aircraft that flies like a helicopter. Technically, it's called an autogyro. The autogyro was invented in 1923 by a Spaniard named Juan de la Cierva, and was the precursor to the helicopter. The air flowing through the blades makes them spin, which creates lift and allows the autogyro to descend slowly. When a helicopter's engine fails, it becomes like an autogyro, and falls slowly to the ground like the Chopper.

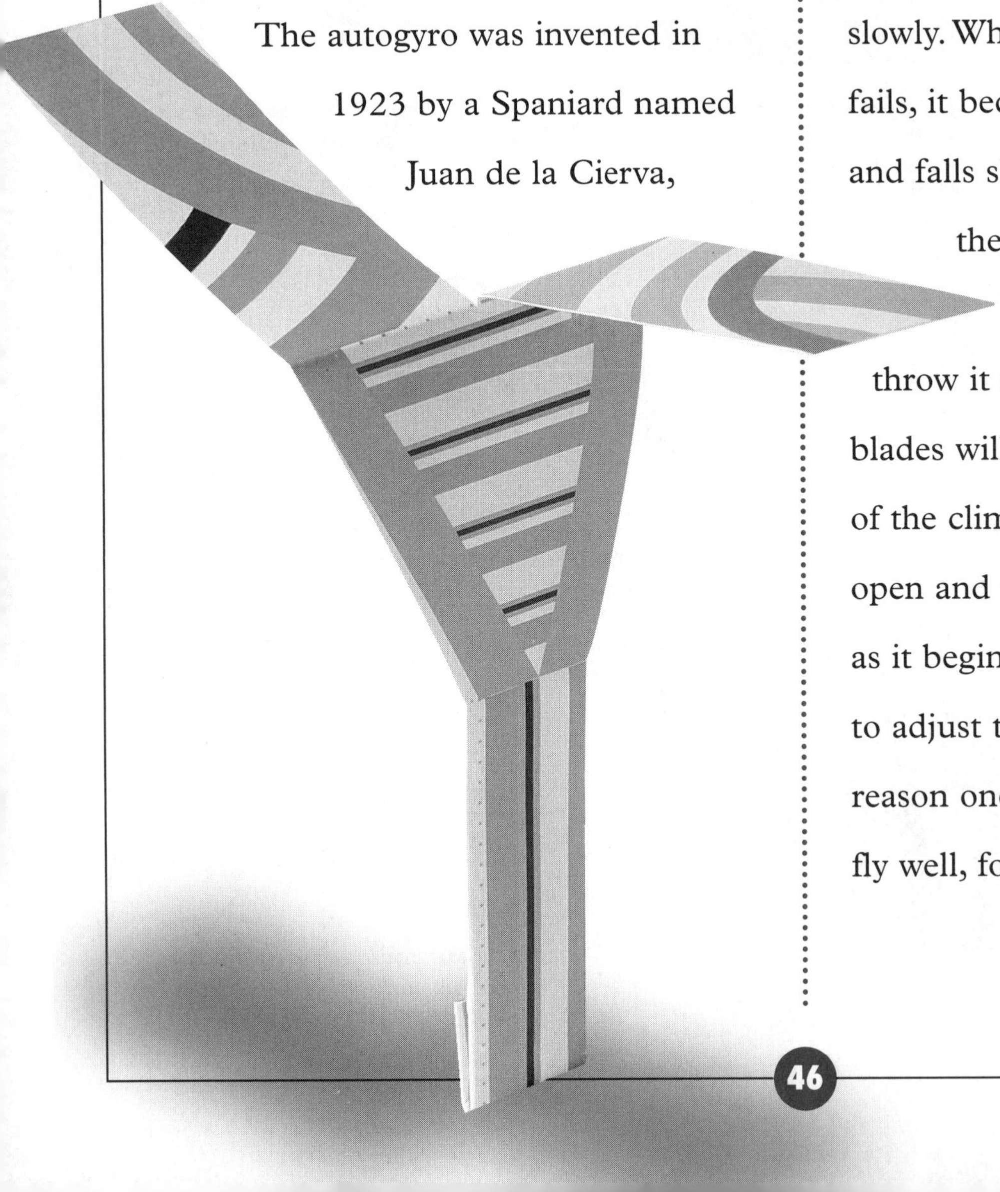

To launch the Chopper, throw it straight up in the air. The blades will remain folded until the top of the climb, at which point they'll open and the craft will spin rapidly as it begins to fall. There's no real way to adjust this aircraft, so if for some reason one of your Choppers doesn't fly well, fold up another.

Remember: Cut on solid black lines; fold in on dashed lines; fold away on dotted lines.

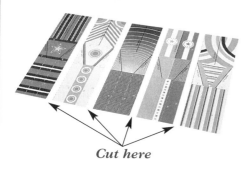

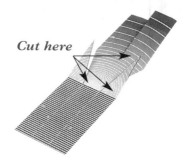

Cut here

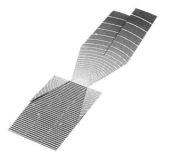

Cut here

1. This sheet makes 5 planes. Cut the choppers apart along solid black lines as shown.

2. Cut along solid black lines as shown.

3. Fold down along lines 1 and 2.

4. Fold in along line 3.

5. Fold in along line 4.

6. Fold up on line 5.

7. Tape as shown (optional).

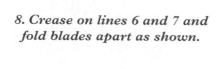

8. Crease on lines 6 and 7 and fold blades apart as shown.

THE INTERCEPTOR

THE INTERCEPTOR IS A GOOD example of how you can experiment with and modify a basic design, in this case the dart. The Interceptor's nose is a little heavier than most darts', making the plane more stable. It's also exceptionally good for both distance and accuracy.

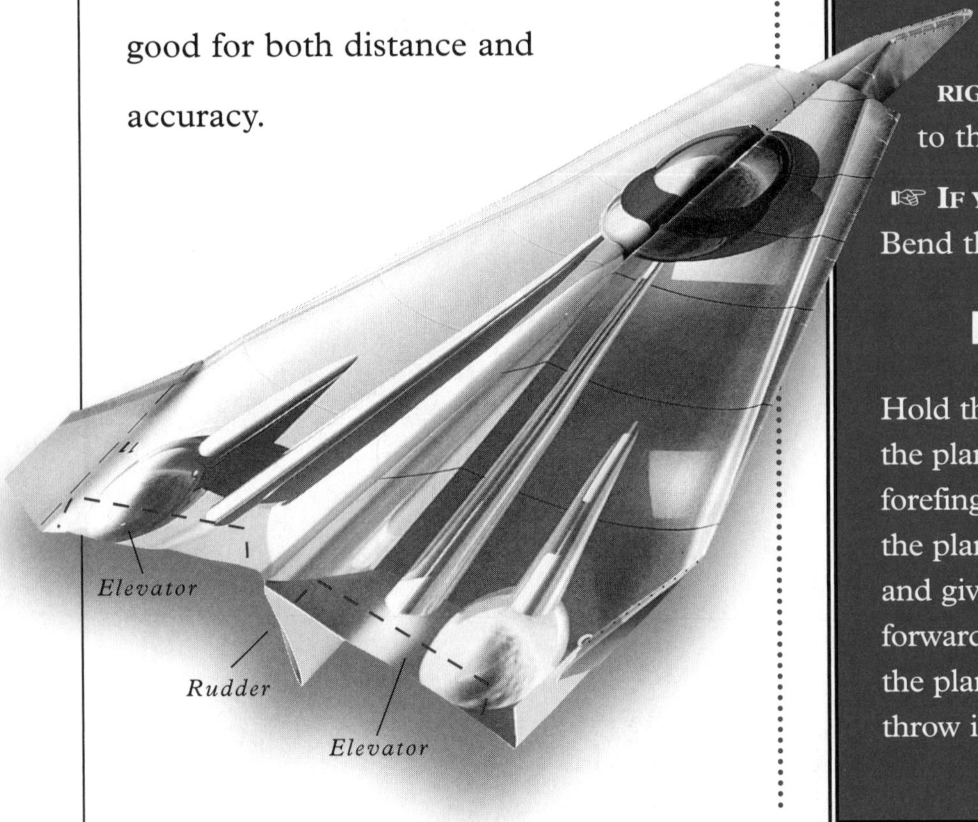

Elevator

Rudder

Elevator

FLIGHT ADJUSTMENTS

☞ **IF YOUR PLANE DIVES:** Bend the elevators up a little *or* throw the plane a little faster.

☞ **IF YOUR PLANE CLIMBS, SLOWS, THEN DIVES:** Bend the elevators down a little *or* throw the plane a little slower.

☞ **IF YOUR PLANE VEERS RIGHT:** Bend the rudder a little to the left.

☞ **IF YOUR PLANE VEERS LEFT:** Bend the rudder a little to the right.

BEST-BET THROW

Hold the fuselage toward the front of the plane between your thumb and forefinger. For shorter flights, hold the plane in front of your shoulder and give it a gentle, level push forward. For longer flights, hold the plane above your shoulder and throw it faster and a little upward.

Remember: Fold in on dashed lines; fold away on dotted lines.

1. Fold along centerline, fold 7, and reopen.

2. Flip plane over and fold along lines 1 and 2.

3. Fold along lines 3 and 4.

4. Fold nose up on line 5.

5. Fold nose back on line 6.

6. Flip plane over and fold plane in half along centerline, fold 7.

7. Fold wing down along line 8.

8. Flip plane over and fold wing down along line 9.

9. Fold wingtips up along lines 10 and 11.

Bend elevators up slightly for best flight.

Make sure wingtips lie above airplane body so wings form a slight "Y" shape with body.

THE STRATUS

THIS GLIDER NOT ONLY LOOKS LIKE a sailplane, it flies like one, too. Like its engineless real-life counterpart, it relies on an outside source of thrust (in this case your throw, rather than a tow) and its large wings to provide lift and keep it aloft. It glides very well at slow speeds. For spectacular flight, try throwing it from a hill or a building, but avoid windy conditions.

FLIGHT ADJUSTMENTS

☞ **IF YOUR PLANE DIVES:** Bend the elevators up a little *or* throw the plane a little faster.

☞ **IF YOUR PLANE CLIMBS, SLOWS, THEN DIVES:** Bend the elevators down a little *or* throw the plane a little slower.

☞ **IF YOUR PLANE VEERS RIGHT:** Bend the rudder a little to the left.

☞ **IF YOUR PLANE VEERS LEFT:** Bend the rudder a little to the right.

BEST-BET THROW

Hold the fuselage toward the front of the plane between your thumb and forefinger at about shoulder height. Push plane forward and slightly downward gently but firmly.

Elevators

Rudder

Remember: Cut on solid red lines; fold in on dashed lines; fold away on dotted lines.

1. Cut along the solid red lines as shown.

2. Fold one wing along lines 1 and 2.

3. Fold other wing along lines 3 and 4.

4. Nest wings to white lines indicated, and tape together on top and bottom.

5. Fold fuselage in half along line 5.

6. Fold down wing tabs along lines 6 and 7 and tail along lines 8 and 9.

7. Tape wing tabs to center of wing on white lines indicated.

8. Bend winglets up along lines 10 and 11. Add a paper clip to the nose for extra stability.

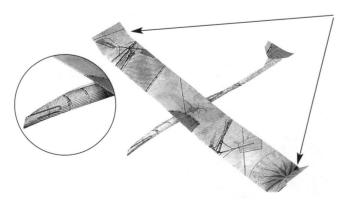

THE VORTEX

THIS PLANE LOOKS TOO SIMPLE TO fly, but you will be surprised. It may be a little difficult to throw at first, but it's a lot of fun once you master it. To launch it, hold it gently around the front of the craft (the heavy end) and throw briskly forward. Let the plane roll off your fingertips as you release it so that it spins like a football (this one is a natural for quarterbacks). Remember, a good spin is key to a great flight.

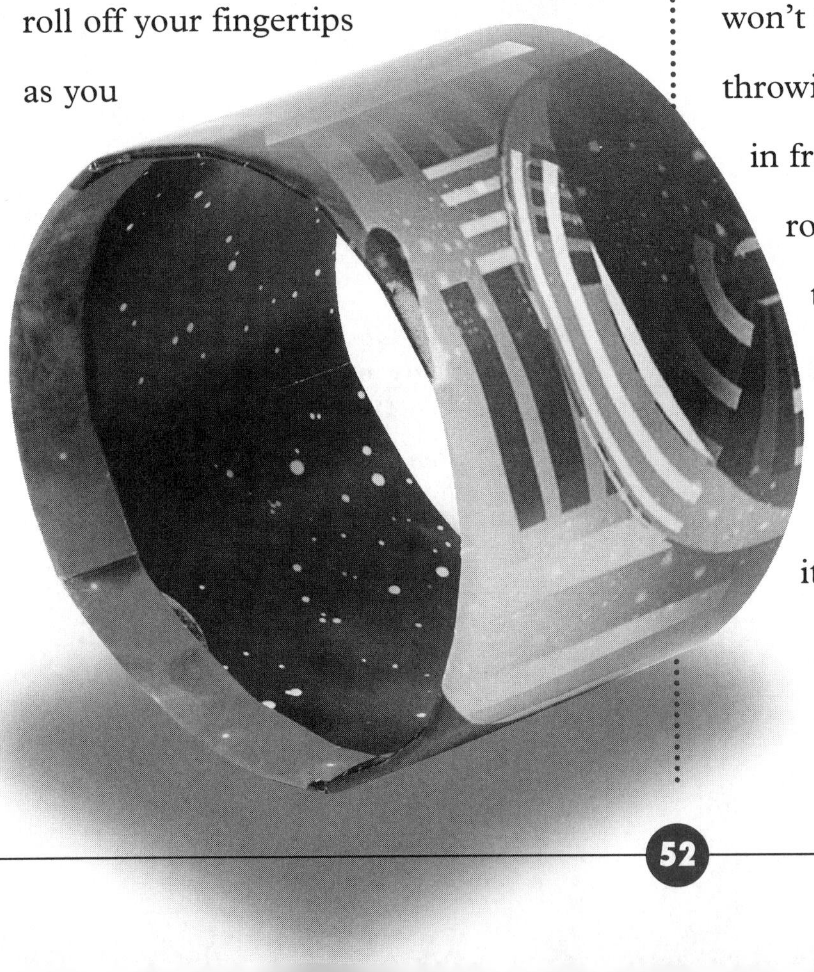

There are only a few ways to adjust this aircraft once it's completed. If you find yourself with a Vortex that won't fly and you're sure that you're throwing it correctly, hold the aircraft in front of you and make sure it's round and not warped. You can also try adding a layer of tape around the front of the tube to make its nose heavier, thereby adding stability. If it still doesn't fly, then it's time to fold up a new Vortex.

Remember: Cut on solid blue lines; fold in on dashed lines; fold away on dotted lines.

← *Cut here*

1. This sheet makes two planes. Cut planes apart along solid blue line, as shown.

2. Fold along line 1 to line 2.

3. Fold along line 2 to line 3, line 3 to line 4.

4. Fold up along line 4.

5. Roll plane into tube with folds on the inside. (Tip: Use your fingers to smooth the tube and to give the plane the right shape.) Interlock edges of fold to hold together. Tape as shown.

THE SHUTTLE

THIS IS A SIMPLE REPLICA OF NASA Shuttle Atlantis (Orbiter Vehicle 104, or OV-104). Atlantis was the fourth of five shuttles built, making its first trip into space on October 3rd, 1985. Like a real shuttle, it is well suited for accuracy, but unlike one, it lacks the strength for long-distance throws. It is very pitch stable and needs a lot of up elevator to fly well.

FLIGHT ADJUSTMENTS

☞ **IF YOUR PLANE DIVES:** Bend the elevators up a little *or* throw the plane a little faster.

☞ **IF YOUR PLANE CLIMBS, SLOWS, THEN DIVES:** Bend the elevators down a little *or* throw the plane a little slower.

☞ **IF YOUR PLANE VEERS RIGHT:** Bend the rudder a little to the left.

☞ **IF YOUR PLANE VEERS LEFT:** Bend the rudder a little to the right.

BEST-BET THROW

Pinch the throwing tab between your thumb and forefinger. Hold the plane in front of your shoulder and give it a gentle, level push forward.

Elevator

Rudder

Elevator

NASA

United States

USA

Atlantis

Remember: Cut on solid red lines; fold in on dashed lines; fold away on dotted lines.

1. Cut out plane and tail along solid red lines.

2. Fold in half along line 1. Push tail up.

3. Fold one wing along line 2.

4. Flip plane over and fold other wing along line 3.

5. Fold throwing tab down along line 4, then crease along line 5.

6. Flip plane over and fold other throwing tab down along line 6, then crease along line 7.

7. Spread wings and join folding tabs. Tape nose closed as shown.

8. Add up elevator as shown.

THE HAMMERHEAD

THE HAMMERHEAD HAS SMALL wings in the front of the plane, known as canards. It's important to make sure these are even, not warped. They are sensitive to minor adjustments, and it may take a little extra effort to get this plane to fly well, but once you do, you'll find it a good straight performer.

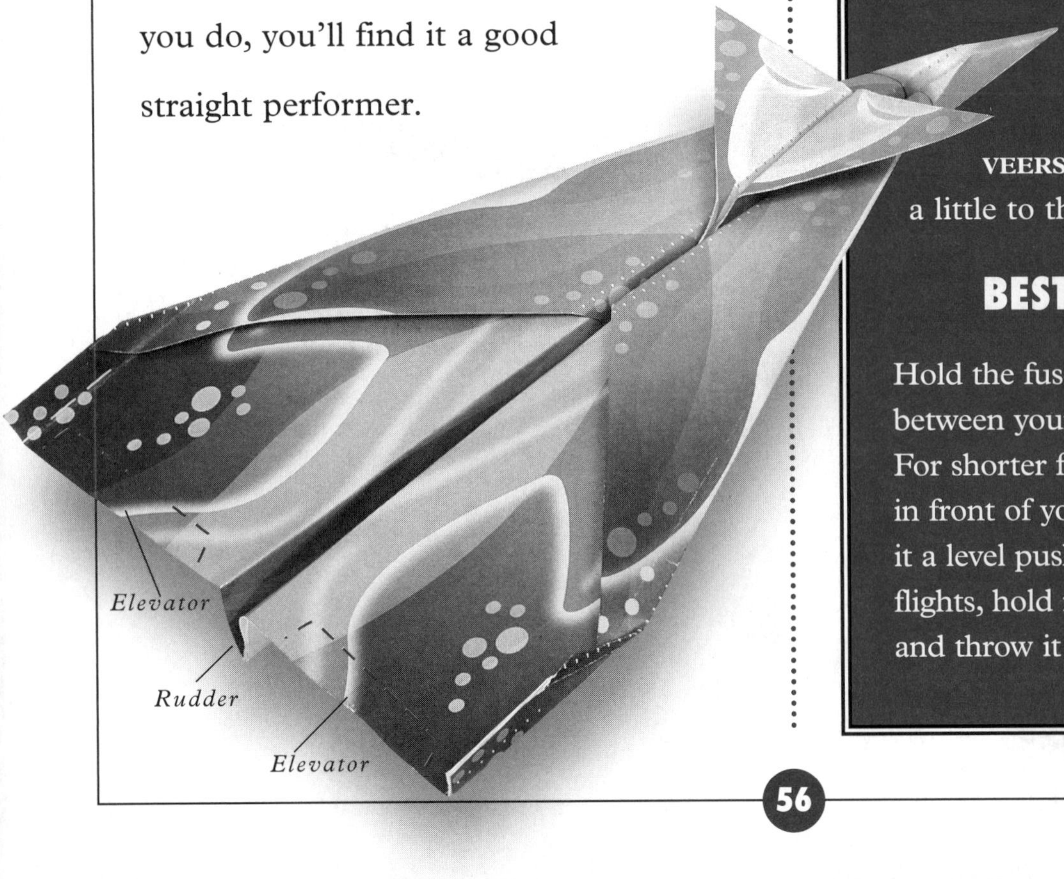

Elevator

Rudder

Elevator

FLIGHT ADJUSTMENTS

☞ **IF YOUR PLANE DIVES:** Bend the elevators up a little *or* throw the plane a little faster.

☞ **IF YOUR PLANE CLIMBS, SLOWS, THEN DIVES:** Bend the elevators down a little *or* throw the plane a little slower.

☞ **IF YOUR PLANE VEERS RIGHT:** Bend the rudder a little to the left.

☞ **IF YOUR PLANE VEERS LEFT:** Bend the rudder a little to the right.

BEST-BET THROW

Hold the fuselage toward the front between your thumb and forefinger. For shorter flights, hold the plane in front of your shoulder and give it a level push forward. For longer flights, hold it above your shoulder and throw it faster and upward.

Remember: Cut on solid green lines; fold in on dashed lines; fold away on dotted lines.

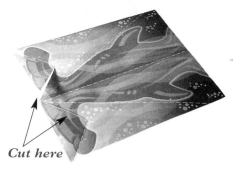

Cut here

1. Cut along solid green lines as shown. Fold along centerline, fold 7 and reopen.

2. Fold along lines 1 and 2.

3. Fold wing in on line 3.

4. Fold back on line 4.

5. Fold other wing in on line 5.

6. Fold back on line 6.

7. Fold plane in half along centerline, fold 7.

8. Fold wing up on line 8 and canard up on line 9.

9. Flip plane over and fold wing down on line 10 and canard on line 11.

10. Fold wingtips up along lines 12 and 13.

Make sure canards are level or slightly down.

Bend elevators up slightly for best flight.

Add paper clip to nose for more stable flight.

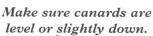

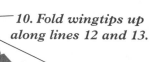

Make sure wingtips lie above airplane body so wings form a slight "Y" shape with body.

THE WORLD RECORD PAPER AIRPLANE

THIS MODEL HAS HELD THE WORLD record for time aloft since 1983. Its longest officially recorded flight took place indoors over a level floor on October 8, 1998, and lasted 27.60 seconds. Outdoors, it can fly very long distances. It's also good at stunts.

Rudders
Elevators

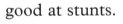

FLIGHT ADJUSTMENTS

☞ **IF YOUR PLANE DIVES:** Bend the elevators up a little *or* throw the plane a little faster.

☞ **IF YOUR PLANE CLIMBS, SLOWS, DIVES:** Bend the elevators down a little *or* throw the plane a little slower.

☞ **IF YOUR PLANE VEERS RIGHT:** Bend the rudder a little to the left.

☞ **IF YOUR PLANE VEERS LEFT:** Bend the rudder a little to the right.

BEST-BET THROW

Hold the fuselage toward the front of the plane between your thumb and forefinger at about shoulder height. Push plane forward and slightly downward gently but firmly. For world record throw, see page 22.

Remember: Fold in on dashed lines; fold away on dotted lines.

1. Fold along lines 1 and 2.

2. Fold along line 3 to line 4.

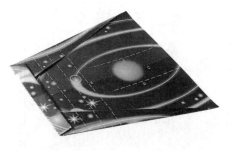

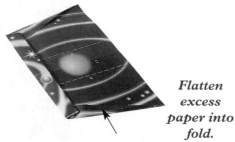

Flatten excess paper into fold.

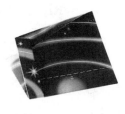

3. Fold along lines 4 through 6.

4. Fold along lines 7 through 10.

5. Flip plane over and fold in half along centerline, fold 11.

6. Fold one wing down along line 12.

7. Flip plane over and fold other wing down along line 13.

8. Fold wingtips up along lines 14 and 15.

Bend elevators up slightly for best flight.

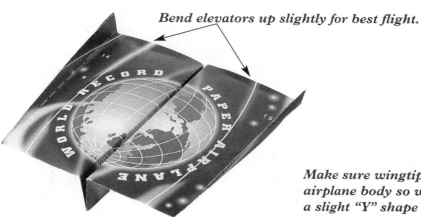

Make sure wingtips lie above airplane body so wings form a slight "Y" shape with body.

THE CAMEL

THIS MODEL WAS INSPIRED BY THE Sopwith Camel, which shot down the Red Baron in World War I. Very popular before the war, by the 1930s, biplanes' popularity decreased because of their excessive drag. That complaint does not apply to this paper version. It may take a little while to make, but it's a good all-around flier.

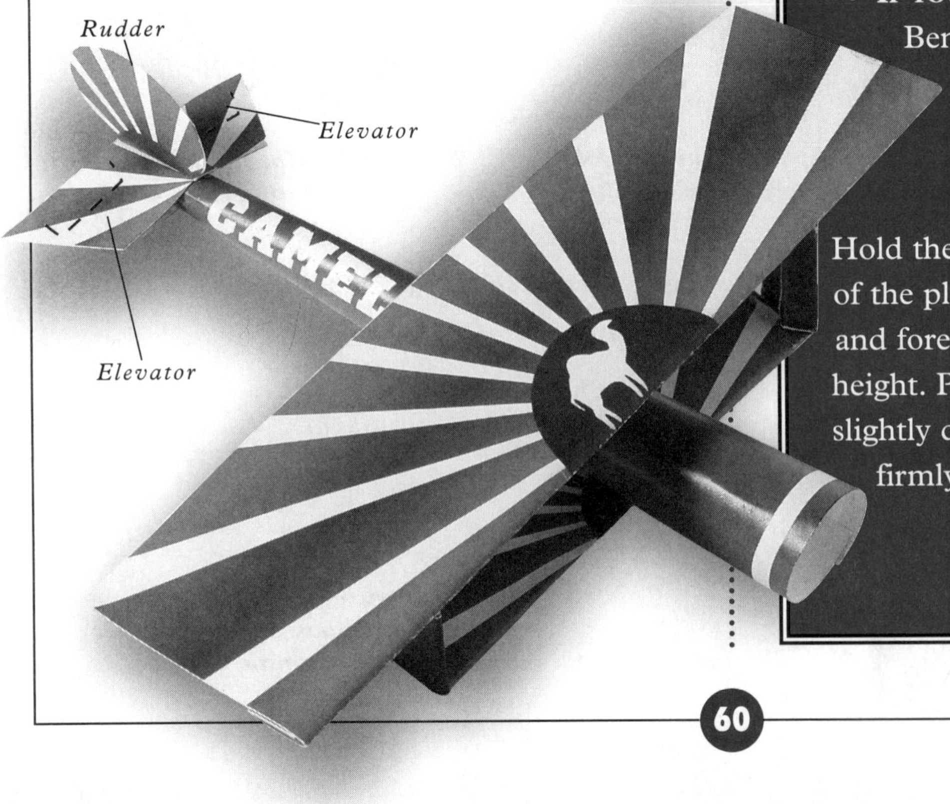

Rudder

Elevator

Elevator

FLIGHT ADJUSTMENTS

☞ **IF YOUR PLANE DIVES:** Bend the elevators up a little *or* throw the plane a little faster.

☞ **IF YOUR PLANE CLIMBS, SLOWS, THEN DIVES:** Bend the elevators down a little *or* throw the plane a little slower.

☞ **IF YOUR PLANE VEERS RIGHT:** Bend the rudder a little to the left.

☞ **IF YOUR PLANE VEERS LEFT:** Bend the rudder a little to the right.

BEST-BET THROW

Hold the fuselage toward the front of the plane between your thumb and forefinger at about shoulder height. Push plane forward and slightly downward gently but firmly.

Remember: Cut on solid black lines; fold in on dashed lines; fold away on dotted lines.

1. Cut sheet apart along solid black lines as shown.

2. Fold top wing along line 1.

3. Fold along lines 2 and 3, and tape as shown.

4. Fold bottom wing along lines 4, 5, and 6.

6. Flip plane over and fold wing supports along lines 11 through 18.

7. Tape lower wing to upper wing as shown, matching up letters. Be sure that the wings are not warped.

5. Fold along lines 7 through 10, wrapping folds 8 and 10 around wing supports, and taping closed.

8. Fold vertical stabilizer on line 19 and tape on both sides to middle of horizontal stabilizer.

9. Crease lightly along lines 20, 21, and 22.

10. Roll fuselage up so that edges overlap slightly, and tape closed.

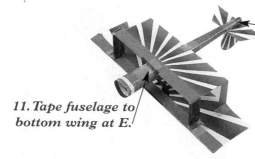

11. Tape fuselage to bottom wing at E.

12. Tape stabilizer to back end of fuselage. Be sure it is centered.

13. Attach one larger or two small paper clips to nose. If using two, place at top and bottom of nose.

THE PHANTOM

THE PHANTOM COMBINES TWO wings with very different sweep angles to create a single wing with a "cranked" leading edge. This design is used on the Saab Draken and will likely be used on supersonic transports in the future because of its low supersonic drag. The Phantom needs up elevator to fly well, and is a good plane for distance and accuracy.

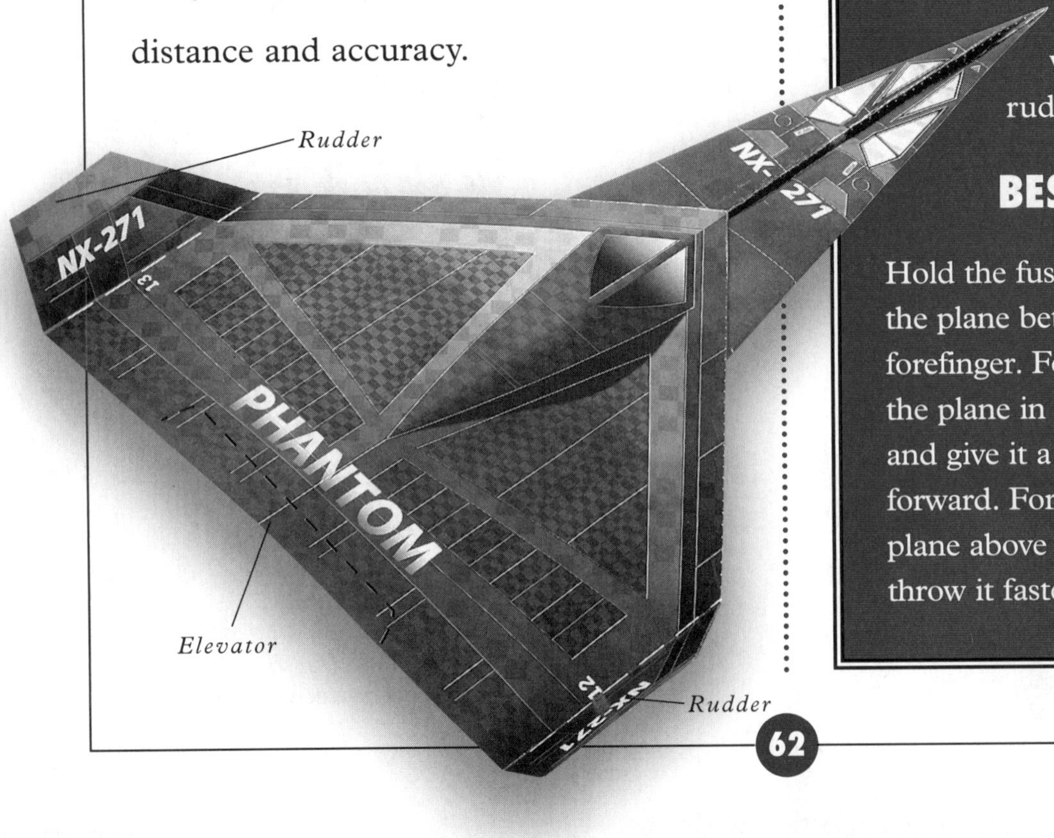

Rudder

Elevator

Rudder

FLIGHT ADJUSTMENTS

☞ **IF YOUR PLANE DIVES:** Bend the elevator up a little *or* throw the plane a little faster.

☞ **IF YOUR PLANE CLIMBS, SLOWS, THEN DIVES:** Bend the elevators down a little *or* throw the plane a little slower.

☞ **IF YOUR PLANE VEERS RIGHT:** Bend the rudder a little to the left.

☞ **IF YOUR PLANE VEERS LEFT:** Bend the rudder a little to the right.

BEST-BET THROW

Hold the fuselage toward the front of the plane between your thumb and forefinger. For shorter flights, hold the plane in front of your shoulder and give it a gentle, level push forward. For longer flights, hold the plane above your shoulder and throw it faster and a little upward.

Remember: Cut on solid blue line; fold in on dashed lines; fold away on dotted lines.

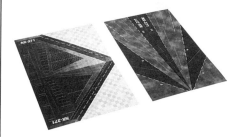

1. Cut sheet apart along solid blue line as shown.

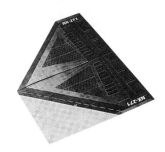

2. Fold wing along line 1.

3. Fold wing along line 2.

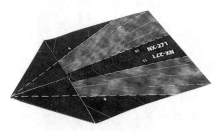

4. Fold dart along lines 3 and 4.

5. Fold along lines 5 and 6, and tape folds closed as shown.

6. Fold along lines 7 and 8.

7. Flip dart over and fold in half along centerline, fold 9.

8. Fold one wing up along line 10.

9. Flip plane over and fold down along line 11.

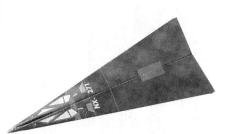

10. Tape top of dart closed.

11. Tape dart to bottom of wing as shown.

12. Tape top of wing to dart as shown. Fold wingtips up on lines 12 and 13. Bend to approximately 45° angles.

THE GALACTICA

THE GALACTICA IS DIFFERENT from most paper airplanes because it doesn't have a body to hold for launching. The good news is, this reduces drag for better flights. It's an excellent glider, especially if you use a little up elevator. It's good for both straight, long-distance flights and graceful circles around the room (see page 29 for tips on aerobatics).

FLIGHT ADJUSTMENTS

☞ **IF YOUR PLANE DIVES:** Bend the elevators up a little *or* throw the plane a little faster.

☞ **IF YOUR PLANE CLIMBS, SLOWS, THEN DIVES:** Bend the elevators down a little *or* throw the plane a little slower.

☞ **IF YOUR PLANE VEERS RIGHT:** Bend the rudder a little to the left.

☞ **IF YOUR PLANE VEERS LEFT:** Bend the rudder a little to the right.

BEST-BET THROW

For best flying results, hold the plane by the thicker triangle of paper on the bottom at shoulder height and give it a gentle, level push forward.

Rudder

Elevator

Rudder

Remember: Fold in on dashed lines; fold away on dotted lines.

1. Fold along line 1 (make a sharp crease) and reopen.

2. Fold along line 2 (make a sharp crease) and reopen.

3. Flip plane over and fold along line 3 (make a sharp crease) and reopen.

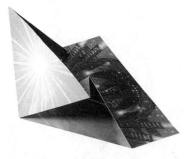

4. Flip plane over and bring points A and B together.

5. Fold as shown.

6. Fold along lines 4 and 5.

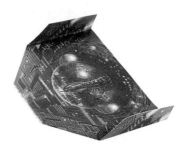

7. Fold nose up along line 6.

8. Fold flaps in along lines 7 and 8. Tuck each flap into a pocket of the nose triangle.

9. Flip plane over and fold along lines 9 and 10 to form wings.

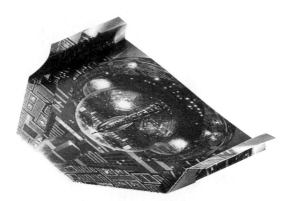

10. Fold wingtips along lines 11 and 12.

THE VALKYRIE

THIS PLANE IS FORMED BY overlapping two dart-shaped wings. It's named after the XB-70 Valkyrie, a 2,000-miles-per-hour experimental bomber tested in the 1960s. The plane's delta wing is very similar to that of its namesake. For most flying, a little up elevator is needed. You'll find this a good plane for both distance and accuracy.

Elevators

Rudder

FLIGHT ADJUSTMENTS

☞ **IF YOUR PLANE DIVES:** Bend the elevators up a little *or* throw the plane a little faster.

☞ **IF YOUR PLANE CLIMBS, SLOWS, THEN DIVES:** Bend the elevators down a little *or* throw the plane a little slower.

☞ **IF YOUR PLANE VEERS RIGHT:** Bend the rudder a little to the left.

☞ **IF YOUR PLANE VEERS LEFT:** Bend the rudder a little to the right.

BEST-BET THROW

Hold the fuselage toward the front of the plane between your thumb and forefinger. For shorter flights, hold the plane in front of your shoulder and give it a gentle, level push forward. For longer flights, hold the plane above your shoulder and throw it faster and a little upward.

Remember: Cut on solid black lines; fold in on dashed lines; fold away on dotted lines.

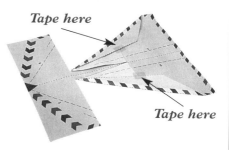

Tape here

Tape here

Cut here

1. Crease along centerline, fold 9, and reopen. Cut along solid black lines.

2. Fold along lines 1 and 2.

3. Fold along lines 3 and 4. Tape as shown.

Tape here

4. Fold along lines 5 and 6.

5. Fold along lines 7 and 8. Tape folds closed as shown.

6. Flip plane over and fold in half along centerline, fold 9.

7. Fold one wing up along line 10.

8. Flip plane over and fold other wing down along line 11.

9. Fold wingtips up along lines 12 and 13.

10. Add up elevator as shown.

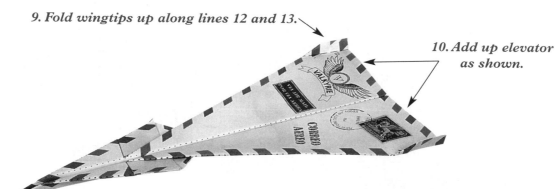

Make sure wingtips lie above airplane body so wings form a slight "Y" shape with body.

THE FALCON

THE FALCON, LIKE ITS FEATHERED namesake, is an excellent glider. It is well suited for time aloft as well as achieving long-distance flights indoors. Outdoors, it is a good choice for launching from both hills and buildings. Try experimenting with different wing sizes and shapes.

Elevators

Rudder

FLIGHT ADJUSTMENTS

☞ **IF YOUR PLANE DIVES:** Bend the elevators up a little *or* throw the plane a little faster.

☞ **IF YOUR PLANE CLIMBS, SLOWS, THEN DIVES:** Bend the elevators down a little *or* throw the plane a little slower.

☞ **IF YOUR PLANE VEERS RIGHT:** Bend the rudder a little to the left.

☞ **IF YOUR PLANE VEERS LEFT:** Bend the rudder a little to the right.

BEST-BET THROW

Hold the fuselage toward the front of the plane between your thumb and forefinger at about shoulder height. Push plane forward and slightly downward gently but firmly.

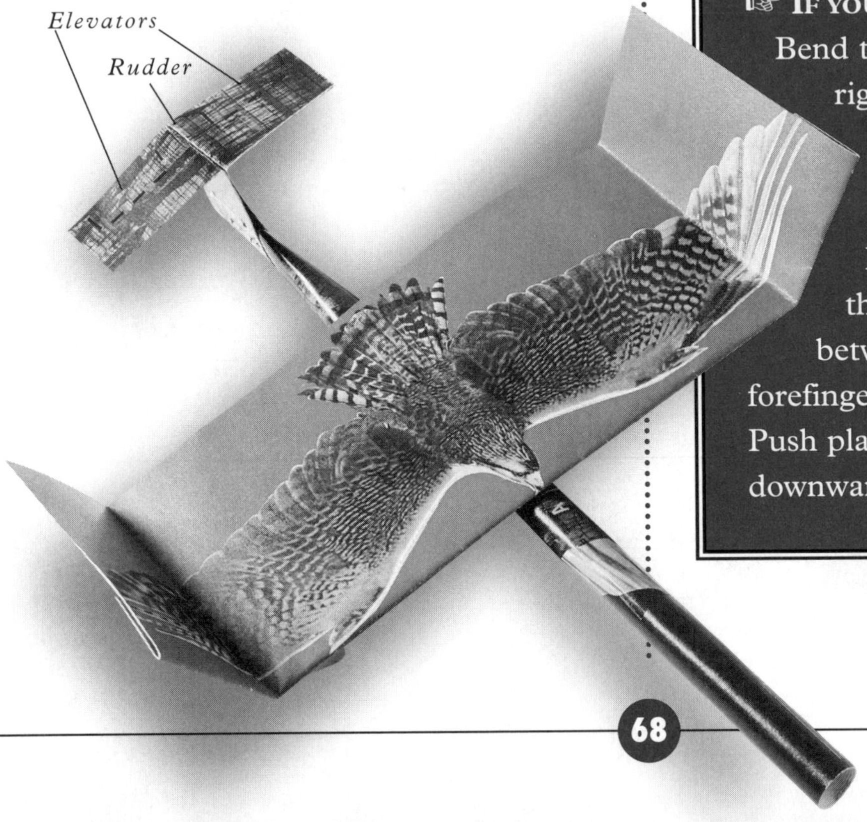

Remember: Cut on solid blue lines; fold in on dashed lines; fold away on dotted lines.

1. Cut sheet apart along solid blue lines as shown.

2. Fold wing along line 1.

3. Fold along lines 2, 3, and 4.

Leading (angled) edge of tail.

4. Fold tail along line 5.

5. Fold along line 6.

6. Flip over and fold along line 7.

7. Roll fuselage in direction of arrow. (Tip: Roll around a pencil.) Try to keep edges even.

8. Tape closed, starting at heavier end.

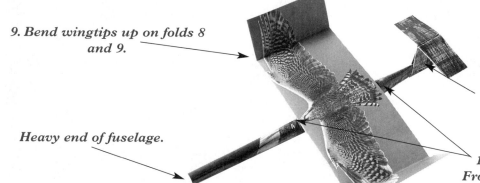

9. Bend wingtips up on folds 8 and 9.

Heavy end of fuselage.

10. Staple tail to lighter end of fuselage. Make sure leading edge faces front.

11. Tape wing to fuselage. Front (folded portion) should be at line A.

THE STILETTO

THE STILETTO IS A SIMPLE PLANE that looks like a very narrow dart. In fact, this design wins many distance and accuracy contests. The slim wings provide lift as well as directional stability. Try experimenting with your Stiletto by adjusting your folds to vary the wing sizes and by adding some up elevator for best flight distance.

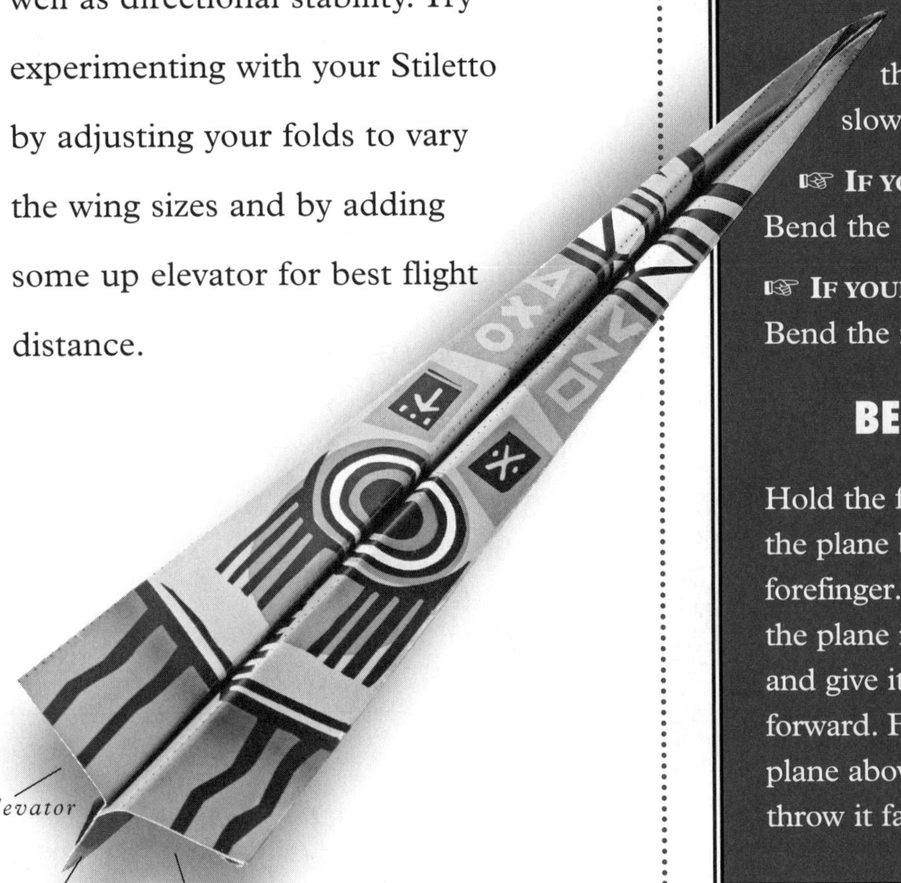

Elevator

Rudder *Elevator*

FLIGHT ADJUSTMENTS

☞ **IF YOUR PLANE DIVES:** Bend the elevators up a little *or* throw the plane a little faster.

☞ **IF YOUR PLANE CLIMBS, SLOWS, THEN DIVES:** Bend the elevators down a little *or* throw the plane a little slower.

☞ **IF YOUR PLANE VEERS RIGHT:** Bend the rudder a little to the left.

☞ **IF YOUR PLANE VEERS LEFT:** Bend the rudder a little to the right.

BEST-BET THROW

Hold the fuselage toward the front of the plane between your thumb and forefinger. For shorter flights, hold the plane in front of your shoulder and give it a gentle, level push forward. For longer flights, hold the plane above your shoulder and throw it faster and a little upward.

Remember: Fold in on dashed lines; fold away on dotted lines.

1. Fold along lines 1 and 2.

2. Fold along lines 3 and 4.

3. Fold along lines 5 and 6.

4. Fold in half along line 7.

5. Fold one wing up along line 8.

6. Flip plane over and fold other wing down along line 9.

Make sure wingtips lie above airplane body so wings form a slight "Y" shape with body.

7. Open as shown.

THE METROPOLIS

LIKE THE FIRST SUCCESSFUL airplane, the Wright Flyer, this plane flies "tail first." Such planes got their nickname "canards" from the French. When the Wright brothers arrived in France, the French thought their plane looked like a duck, and canard is the French word for duck.

To fly properly, this plane requires a lot of down elevator (the opposite of most planes in the book). Try experimenting with the angle of the wingtips.

Elevator

Elevator

Rudders

FLIGHT ADJUSTMENTS

☞ **IF YOUR PLANE DIVES:** Bend the elevators down a bit *or* throw the plane a little faster.

☞ **IF YOUR PLANE CLIMBS, SLOWS, AND DIVES:** Bend the elevators up a bit *or* throw the plane a little slower.

☞ **IF YOUR PLANE VEERS RIGHT:** Bend the rudders a little to the left.

☞ **IF YOUR PLANE VEERS LEFT:** Bend the rudders a little to the right.

BEST-BET THROW

Hold the fuselage toward the front of the plane between your thumb and forefinger at about shoulder height. Push plane forward and slightly downward gently but firmly.

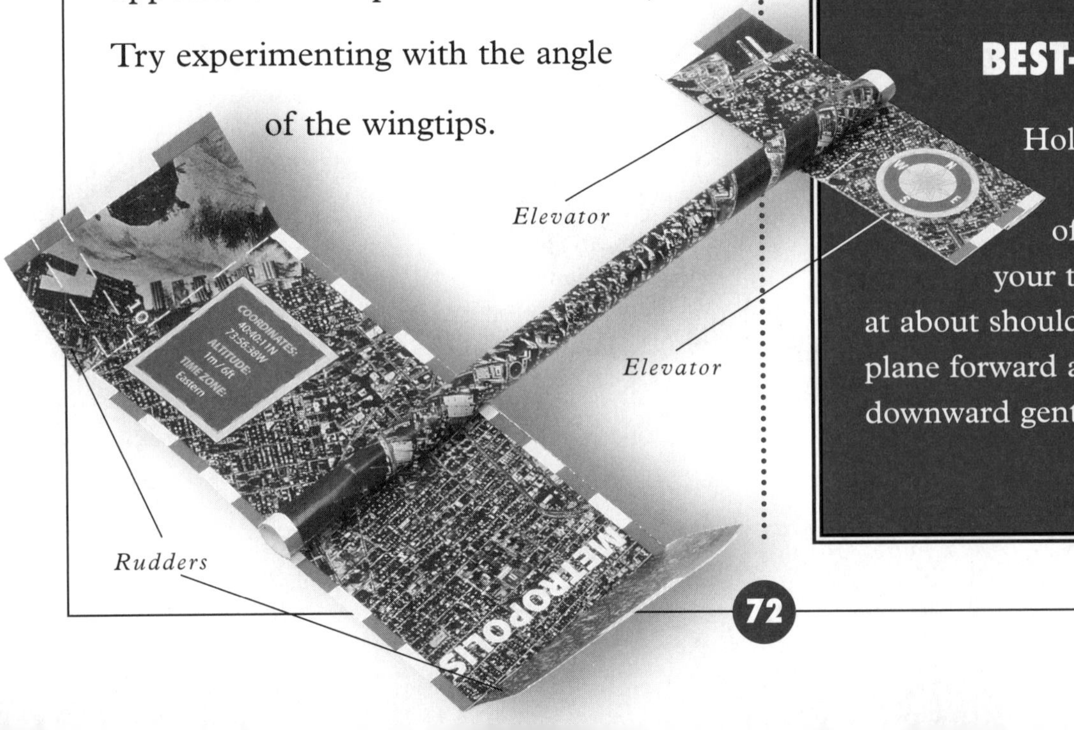

Remember: Cut on solid yellow lines; fold in on dashed lines; fold away on dotted lines.

1. Cut sheet apart along solid yellow lines as shown.

2. Fold along line 1.

3. Fold along lines 2 and 3, and tape as shown.

Cut here

4. Cut sheet as shown. Fold along line 4.

5. Fold along lines 5 through 8, and tape as shown.

6. Roll fuselage in direction indicated. (Tip: Roll around a pencil.) Try to keep edges even.

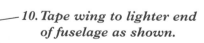

7. Tape closed starting at heavier end.

8. Flatten fuselage about one inch from each end.

11. Bend wingtips up on folds 9 and 10 so they create right angles.

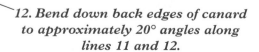

10. Tape wing to lighter end of fuselage as shown.

9. Tape canard to heavy end of fuselage as shown.

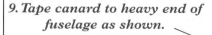

12. Bend down back edges of canard to approximately 20° angles along lines 11 and 12.

THE FLYING WING

THE FLYING WING IS AMONG THE simplest of planes, much like a hang glider. It also resembles the B-2 Spirit stealth bomber. It has weight along the leading edge and a small fuselage. It may need a little up elevator on the trailing edge, but when adjusted properly, it is an excellent glider.

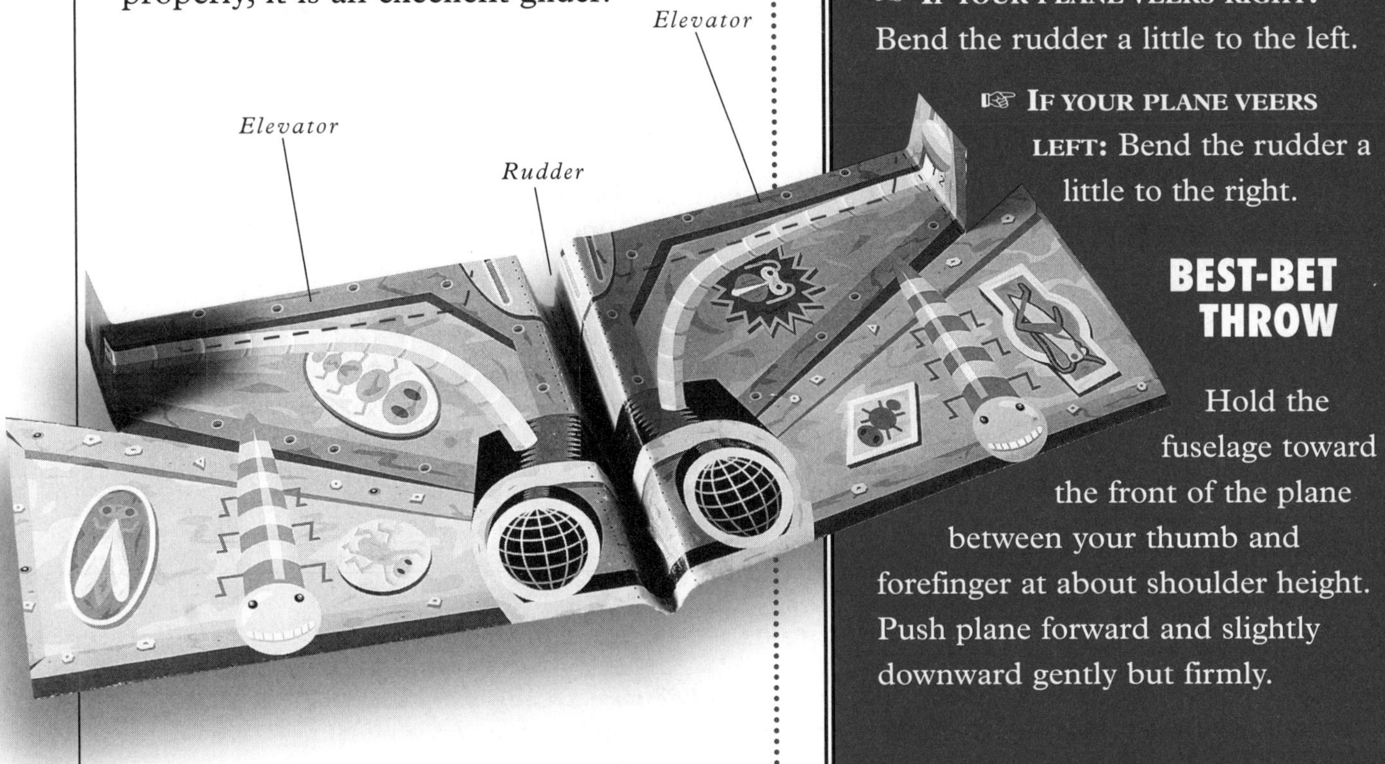

Elevator

Rudder

Elevator

FLIGHT ADJUSTMENTS

☞ **IF YOUR PLANE DIVES:** Bend the elevators up a little *or* throw the plane a little faster.

☞ **IF YOUR PLANE CLIMBS, SLOWS, THEN DIVES:** Bend the elevators down a little *or* throw the plane a little slower.

☞ **IF YOUR PLANE VEERS RIGHT:** Bend the rudder a little to the left.

☞ **IF YOUR PLANE VEERS LEFT:** Bend the rudder a little to the right.

BEST-BET THROW

Hold the fuselage toward the front of the plane between your thumb and forefinger at about shoulder height. Push plane forward and slightly downward gently but firmly.

Remember: Cut on solid orange lines; fold in on dashed lines; fold away on dotted lines.

Cut here →

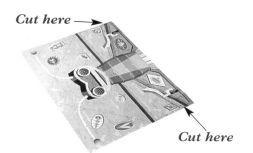

Cut here

1. Cut wingtips along solid orange lines.

2. Fold along lines 1 and 2.

3. Fold along lines 3, 4, and 5.

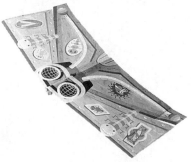

4. Fold along lines 6 through 8.

5. Flip plane over and fold in half along line 9.

6. Fold one wing down along line 10.

7. Flip plane over and fold other wing along line 11.

8. Fold wingtips up along lines 12 and 13.

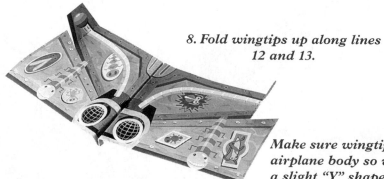

Make sure wingtips lie above airplane body so wings form a slight "Y" shape with body.

THE SPITFIRE

THIS PLANE IS NAMED AFTER THE British Supermarine Spitfire, one of the greatest fighters of World War II. More than 20,000 Spitfires were built, and they are credited by many as the plane that saved England. Your Spitfire may not have such a dramatic role in world history, but it is a superb flyer. Try a mission across the room or down the hall.

Rudder

Elevator

Elevator

FLIGHT ADJUSTMENTS

For normal flight use a little up elevator. This plane's elevator is sensitive, so make your adjustments subtle.

☞ **IF YOUR PLANE DIVES:** Bend the elevators up a little *or* throw the plane a little faster.

☞ **IF YOUR PLANE CLIMBS, SLOWS, THEN DIVES:** Bend the elevators down a little *or* throw the plane a little slower.

☞ **IF YOUR PLANE VEERS RIGHT:** Bend the rudder a little to the left.

☞ **IF YOUR PLANE VEERS LEFT:** Bend the rudder a little to the right.

BEST-BET THROW

Hold the fuselage toward the front between your thumb and forefinger at about shoulder height. Push plane forward and slightly downward gently but firmly.

Remember: Cut on solid green lines; fold in on dashed lines; fold away on dotted lines.

1. Cut end off along solid green line as shown.

2. Fold in on lines 1 and 2.

3. Fold nose up on line 3.

4. Fold body of plane up along line 4.

5. Fold nose down along line 5.

6. Flip plane over and fold in half along line 6.

7. Fold one wing down along line 7.

8. Flip plane over and fold other wing up along line 8.

9. Open plane as shown.

10. Cut tail along solid green line. Push tail up along lines 9 and 10.

Make sure wingtips lie above airplane body so wings form a slight "Y" shape with body.

Flight Log

PILOTS OF FULL-SIZE AIRPLANES use flight logs to track types of planes flown, flight time, and to take notes on interesting trips. You can keep a log of your paper airplane flights for the same reasons. You don't have to make an entry for every flight. This log is best used for recording new types of planes flown, longest time aloft, or greatest distance achieved, and keeping track of how adjustments and modifications affect flight time or distance.

Date	Airplane Type	Location	Longest Time Aloft	Greatest Distance	Remarks	No. of Flights

FLIGHT LOG

Date	Airplane Type	Location	Longest Time Aloft	Greatest Distance	Remarks	No. of Flights

FLIGHT LOG

Date	Airplane Type	Location	Longest Time Aloft	Greatest Distance	Remarks	No. of Flights

The Hangar

The planes themselves

THE BASIC SQUARE

THE BASIC DART

THE STUNT

THE EAGLE

THE CHOPPER

THE INTERCEPTOR

THE STRATUS

THE VORTEX

THE SHUTTLE

THE HAMMERHEAD

**THE WORLD RECORD
PAPER AIRPLANE**

THE CAMEL

THE PHANTOM

THE GALACTICA

THE VALKYRIE

THE FALCON

THE STILETTO

THE METROPOLIS

THE FLYING WING

THE SPITFIRE

BASIC SQUARE

STUNT

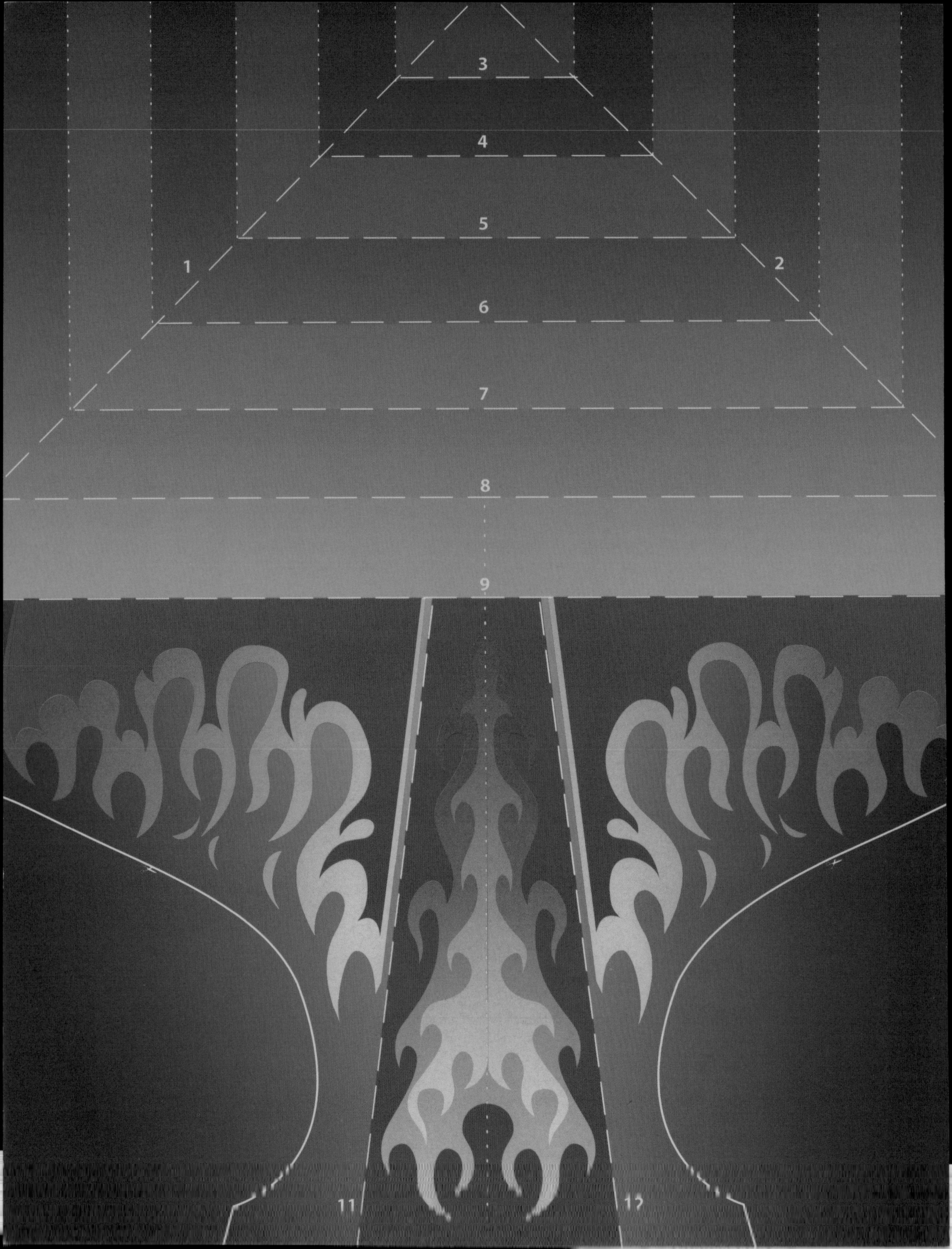
3
4
5
1
2
6
7
8
9
11

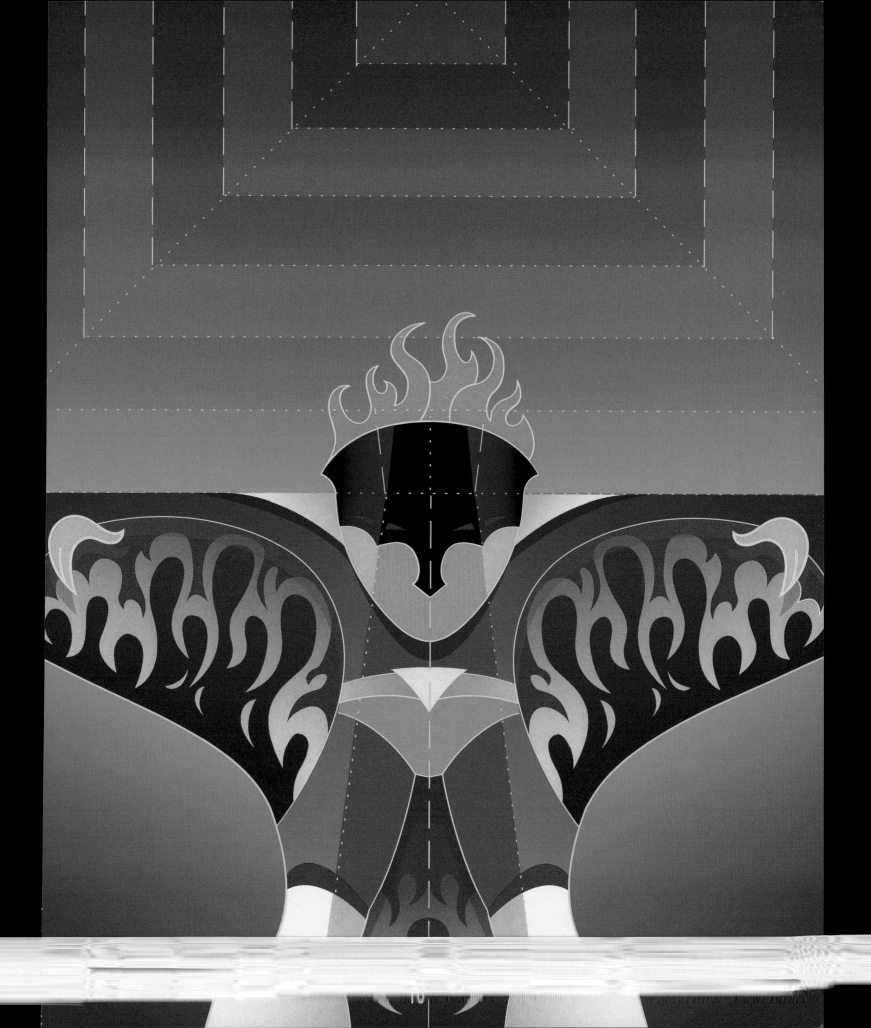

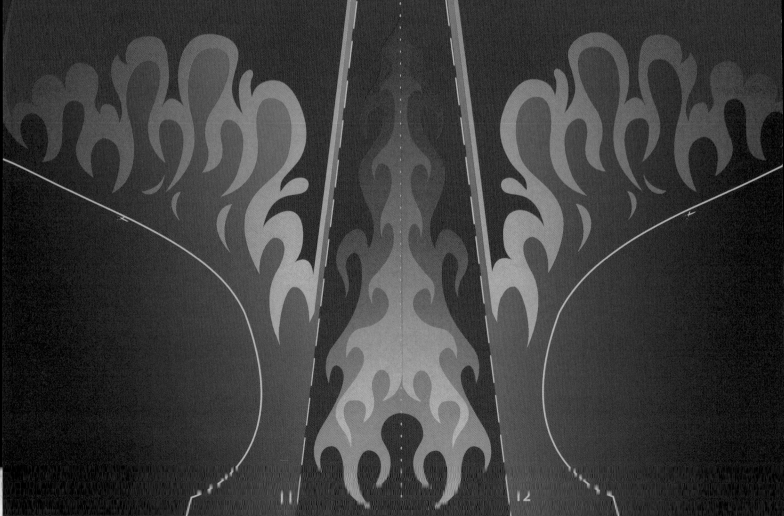

EAGLE

EAGLE

INTERCEPTOR

INTERCEPTOR

STRATUS

4   3   5   1   2

▲ **Overlap wing** ▲
to here

Tape fuselage here

7

6

▲ Overlap wing ▲
to here

9

8

STRATUS

▲ Overlap wing ▲
to here

Tape fuselage here

11

10

7

6

▲ Overlap wing ▲
to here

9

8

STRATUS

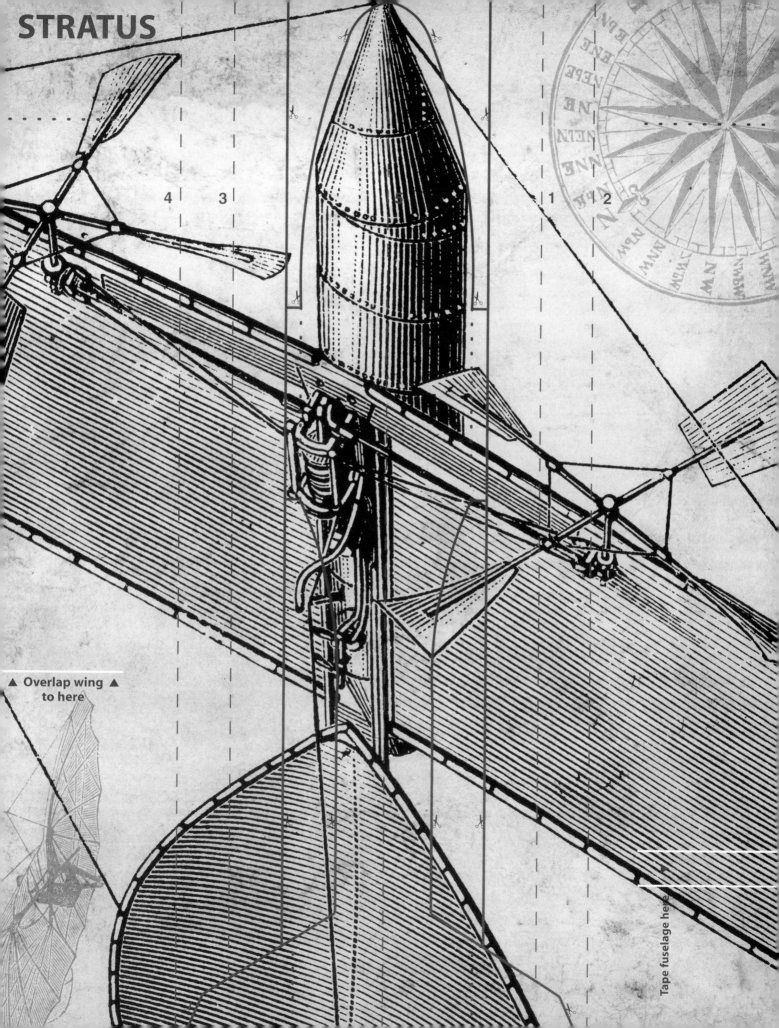

4   3

1   2

▲ **Overlap wing** ▲
to here

Tape fuselage here

11

10

7

6

9

8

Overlap wing
to here

STRATUS

4 3   1 2

▲ Overlap wing ▲
to here

Tape fuselage here

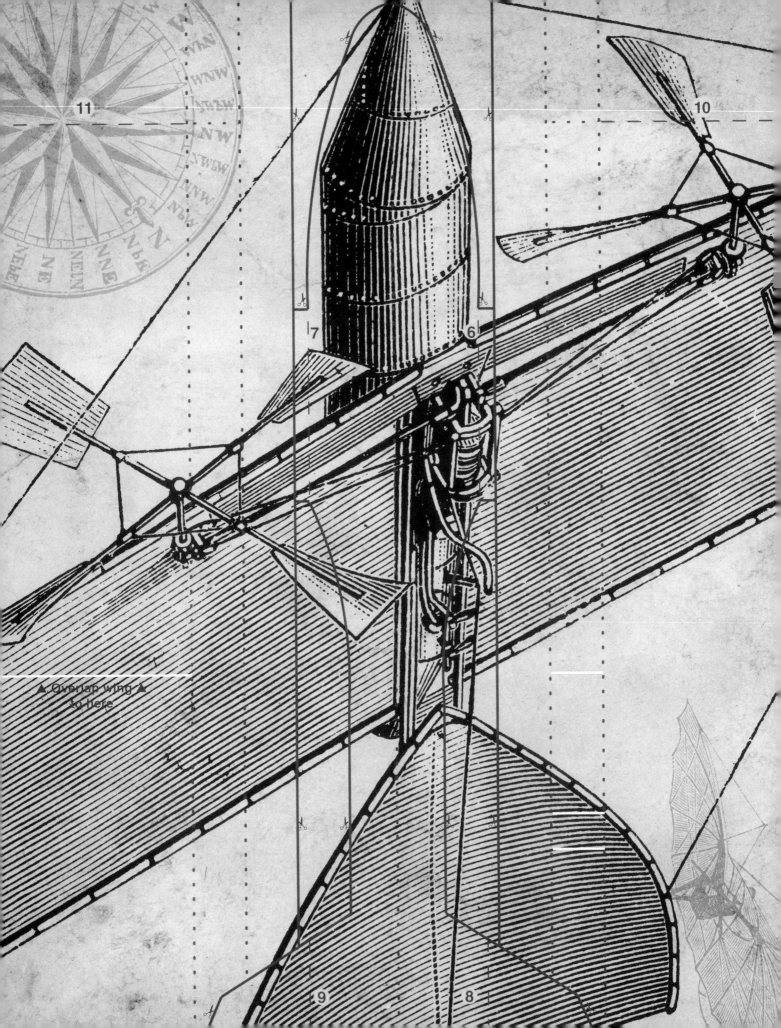

11

10

7

6

▲ Overlap wing ▲
to here

9

8

VORTEX

VORTEX

VORTEX

SHUTTLE

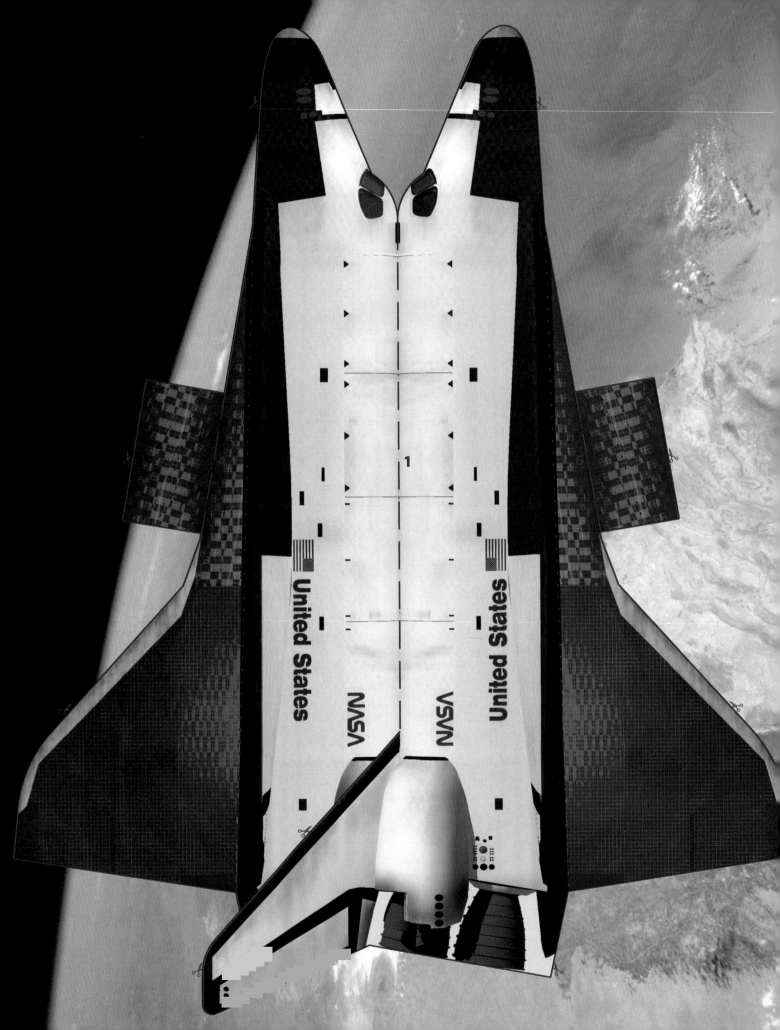

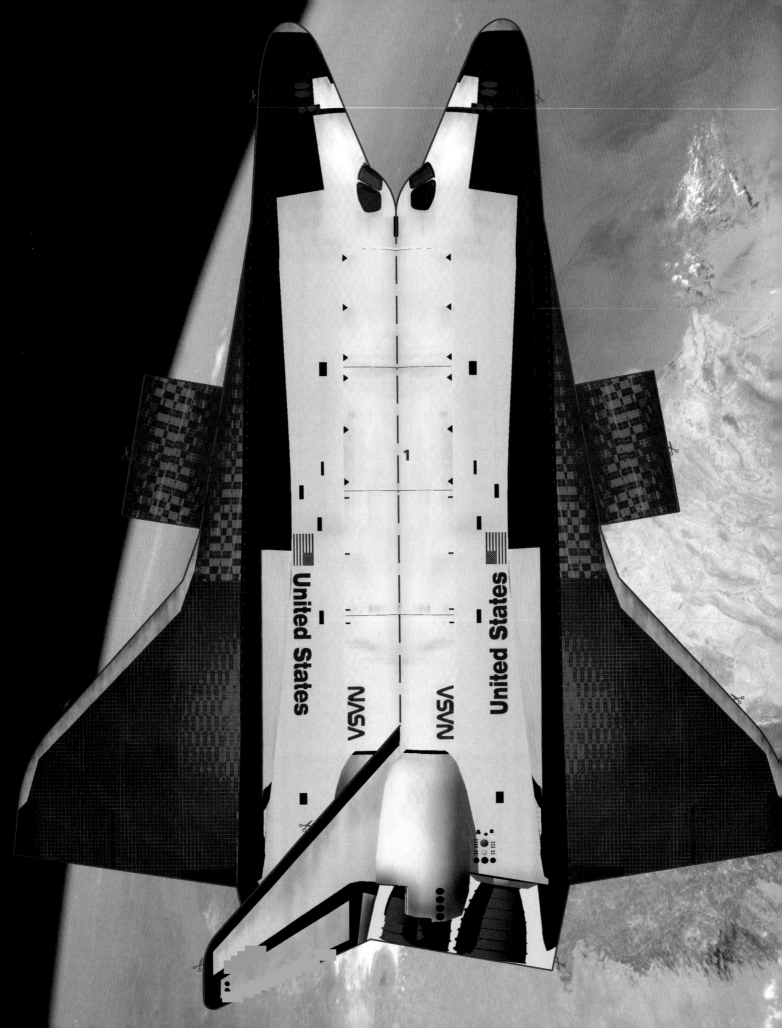

SHUTTLE

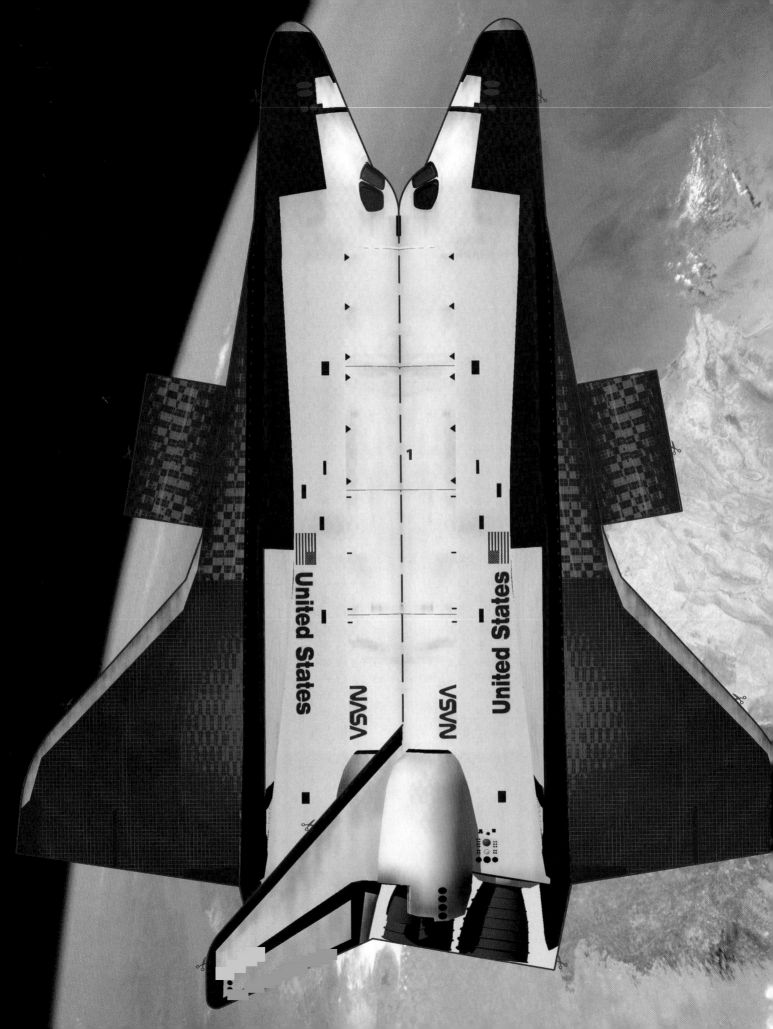

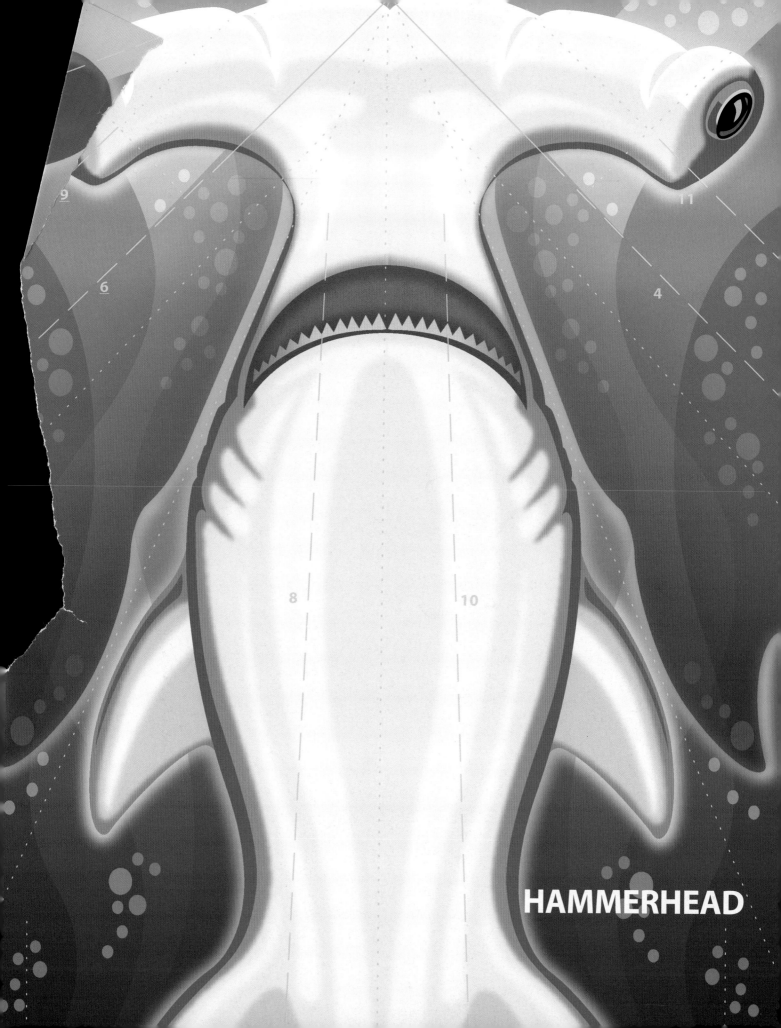

HAMMERHEAD

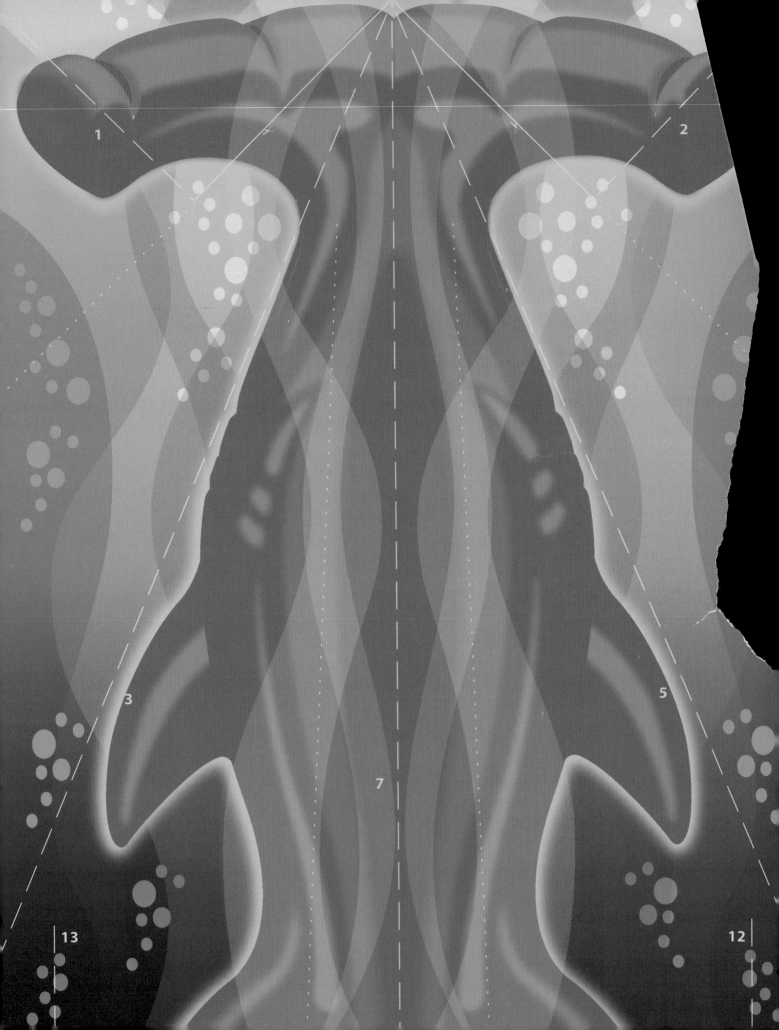

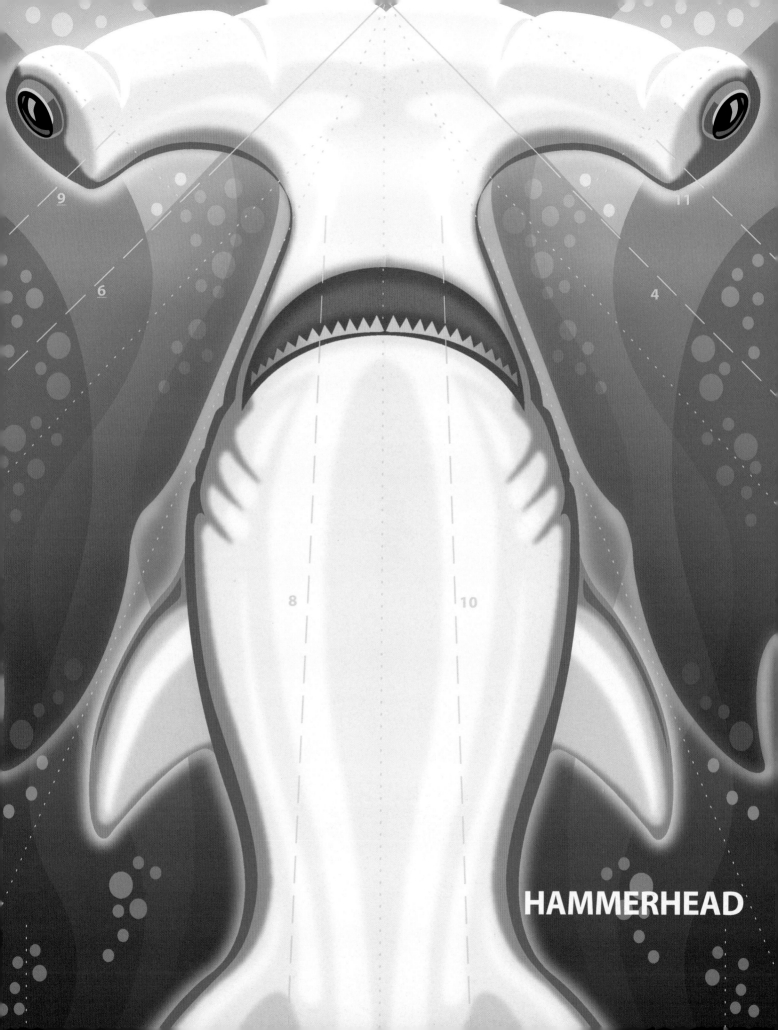

HAMMERHEAD

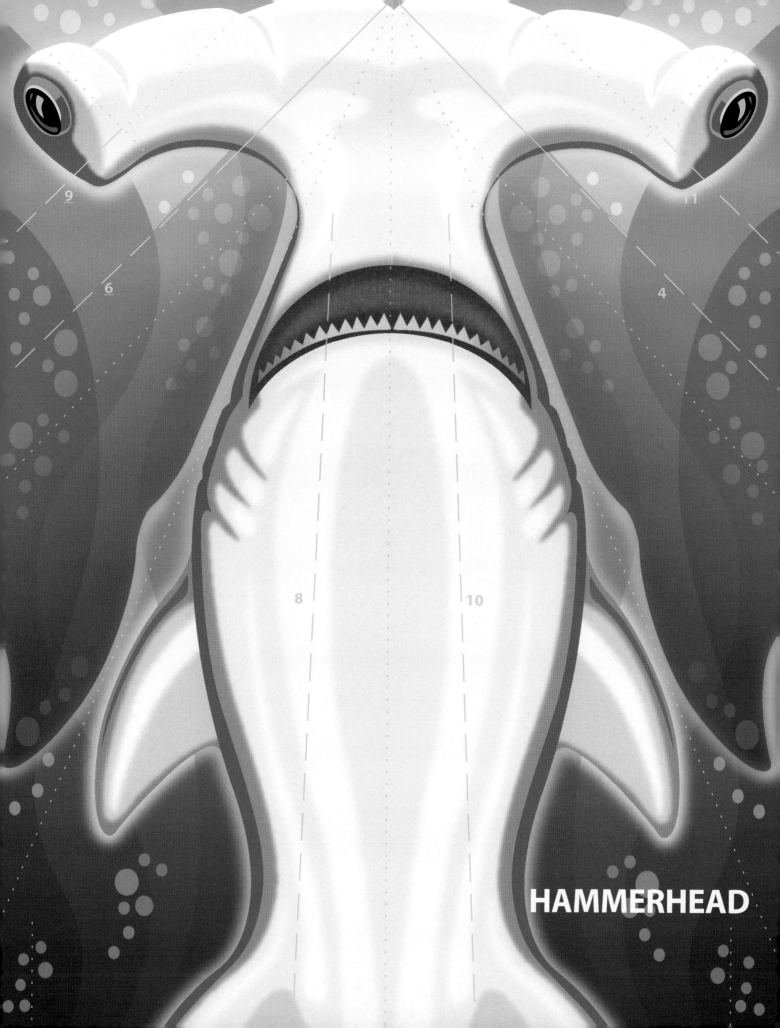

HAMMERHEAD

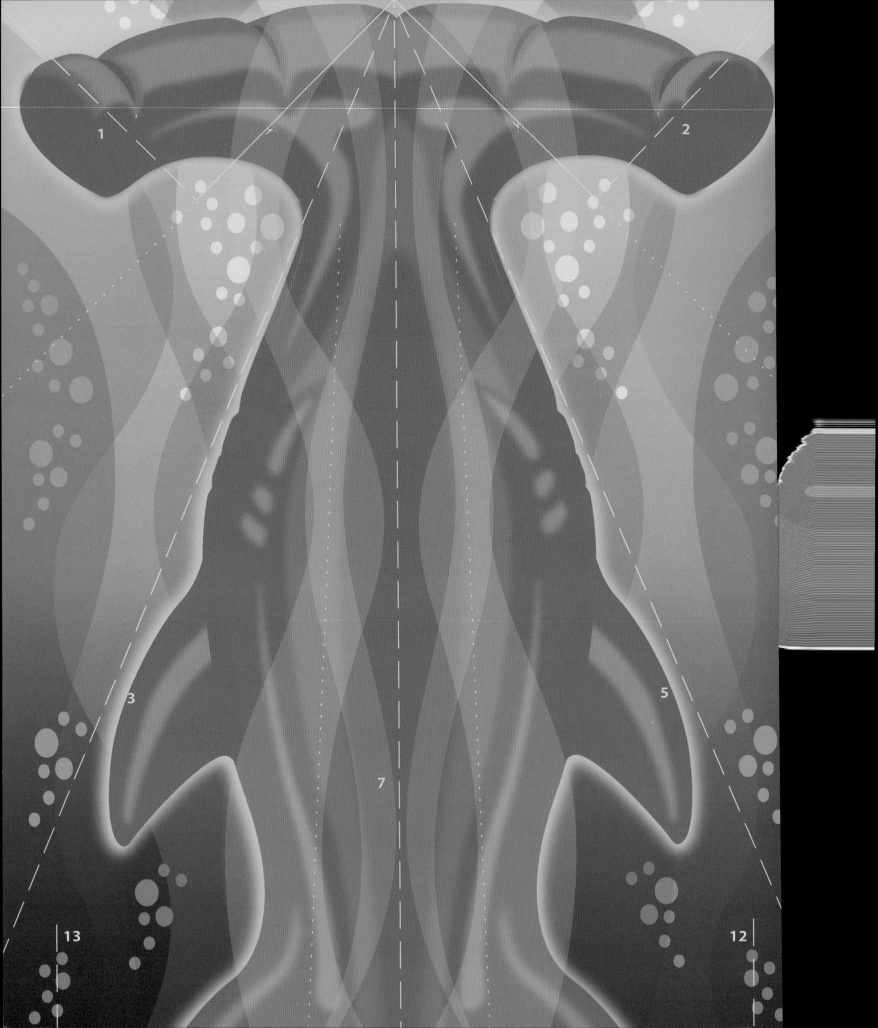

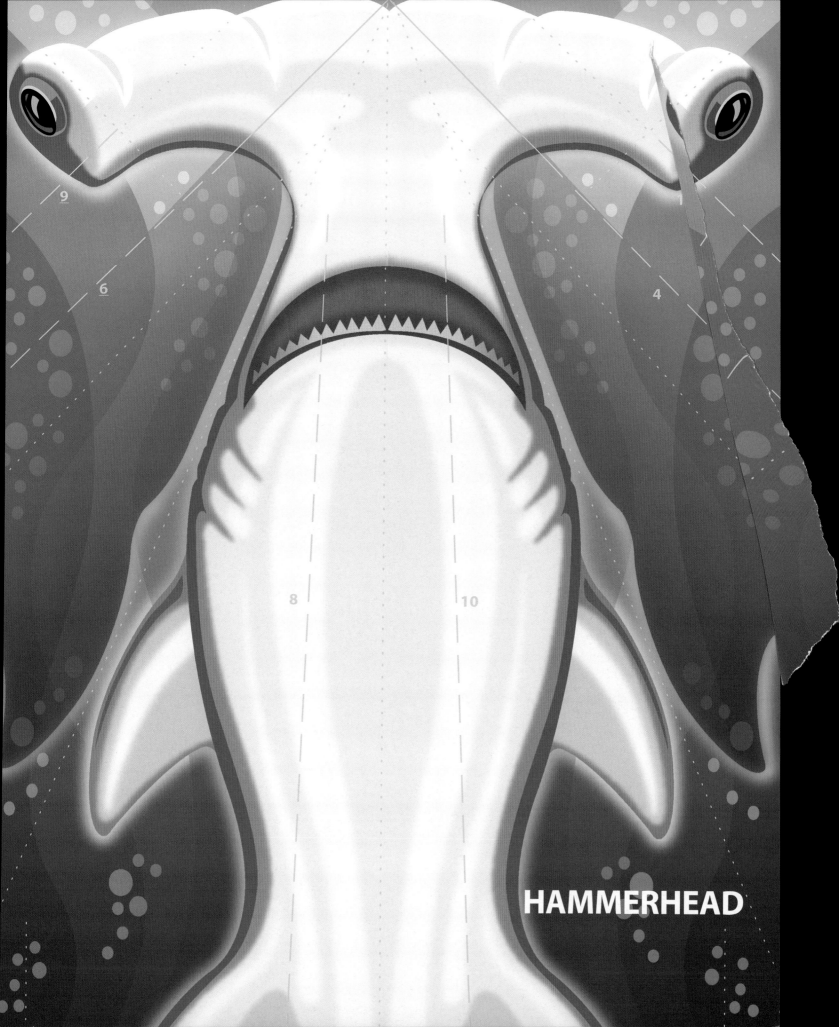

HAMMERHEAD

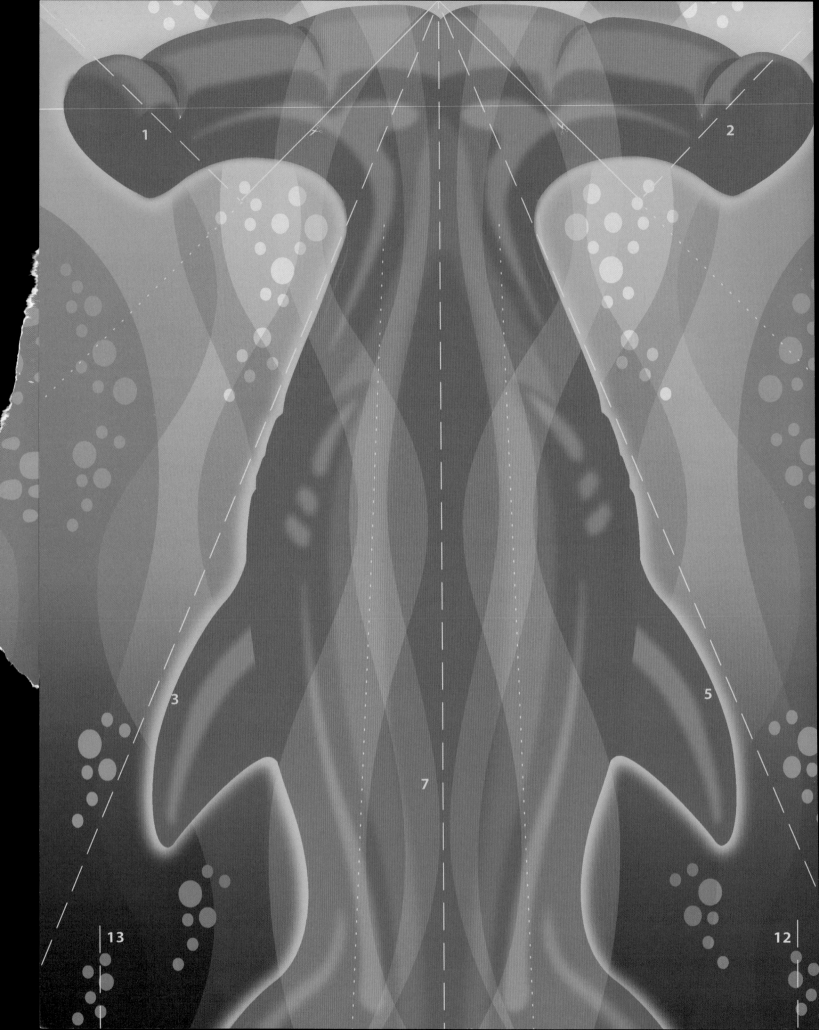

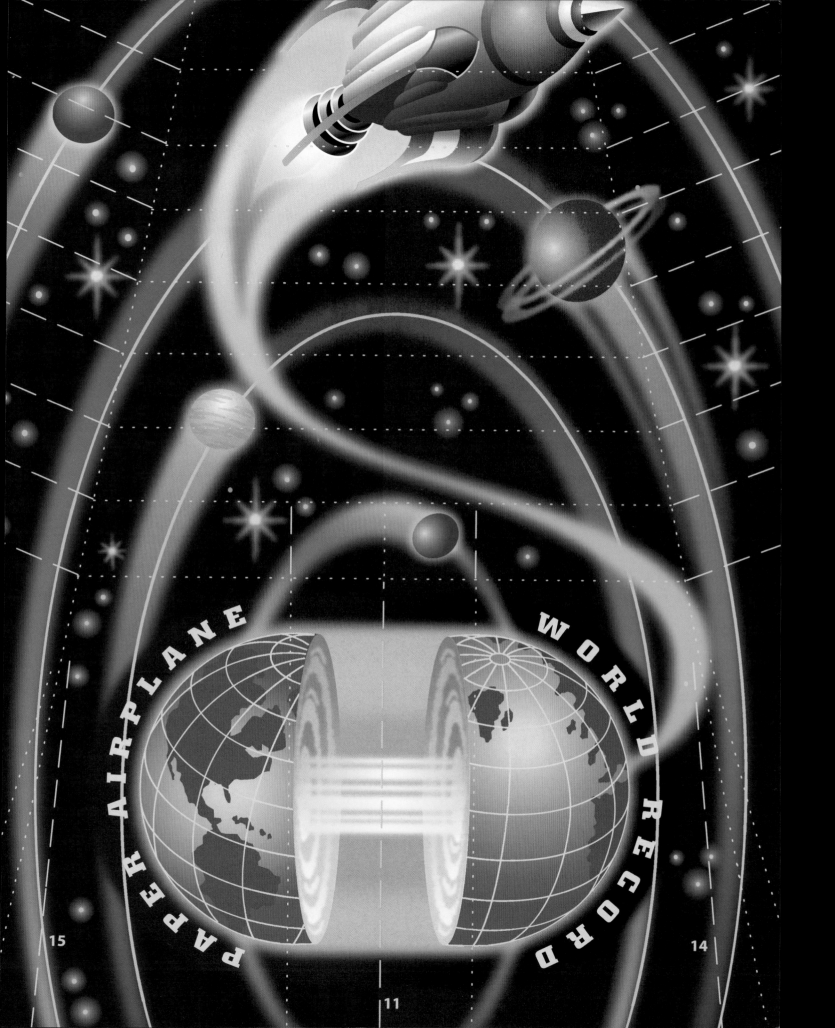

PAPER AIRPLANE WORLD RECORD

PAPER AIRPLANE WORLD RECORD

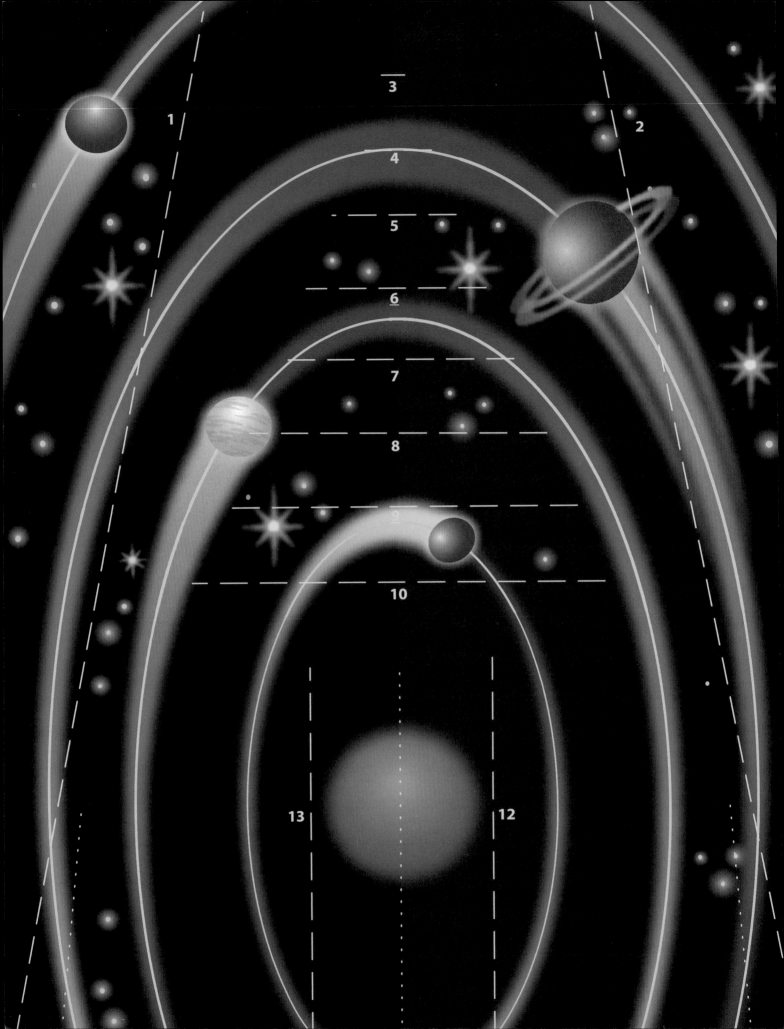

PAPER AIRPLANE WORLD RECORD

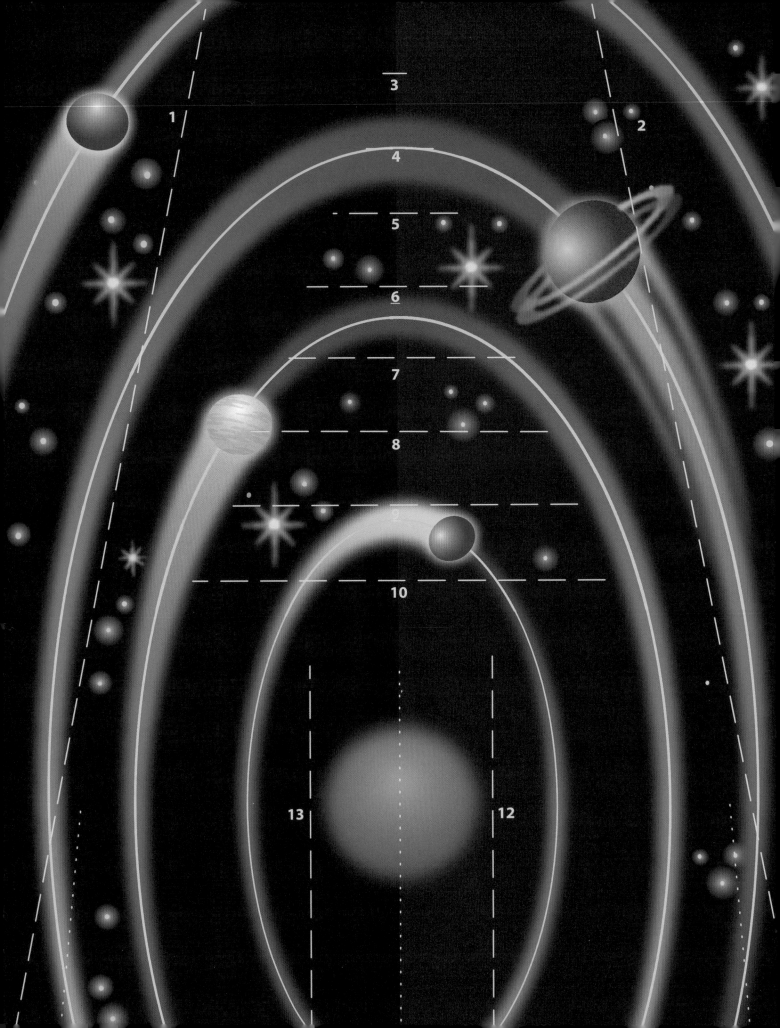

Tape Wing Here

CAMEL

D | C |

14 | 12

13 | 11

Tape Wing

CAMEL

Tape Wing
Here

CAMEL

D

C

14

13

12

11

CAMEL

Tape Wing
Here

CAMEL

D   C

14   12

13   11

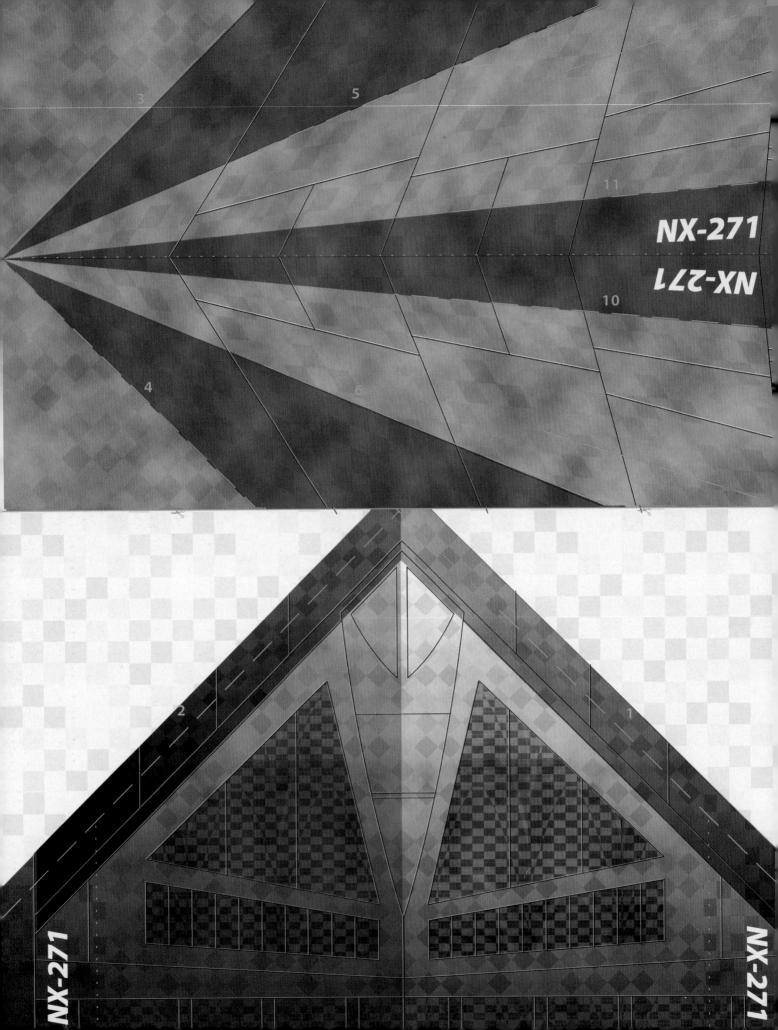

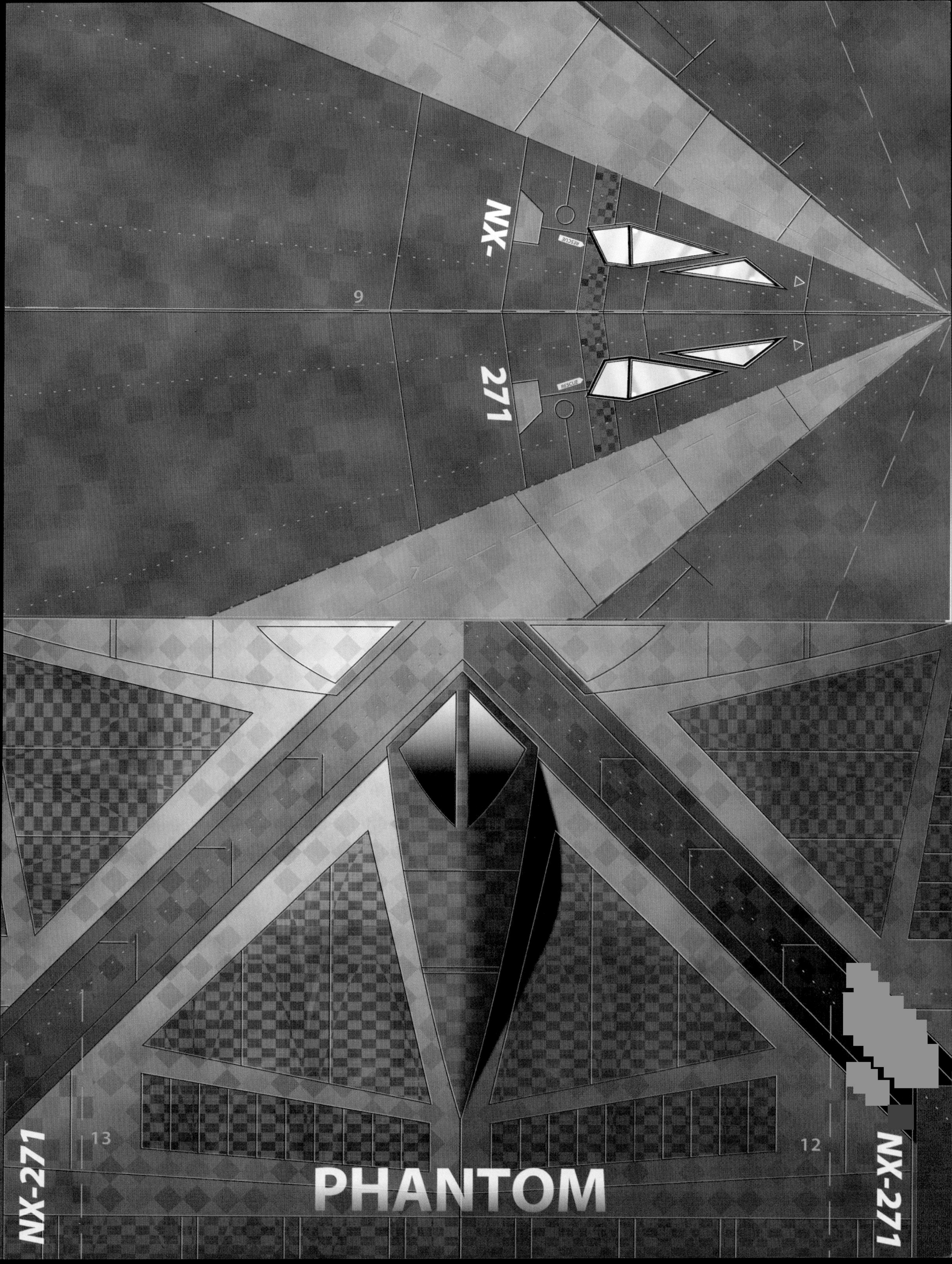
NX-
271
RESCUE
RESCUE
9
7
13
12
PHANTOM
NX-271
NX-271

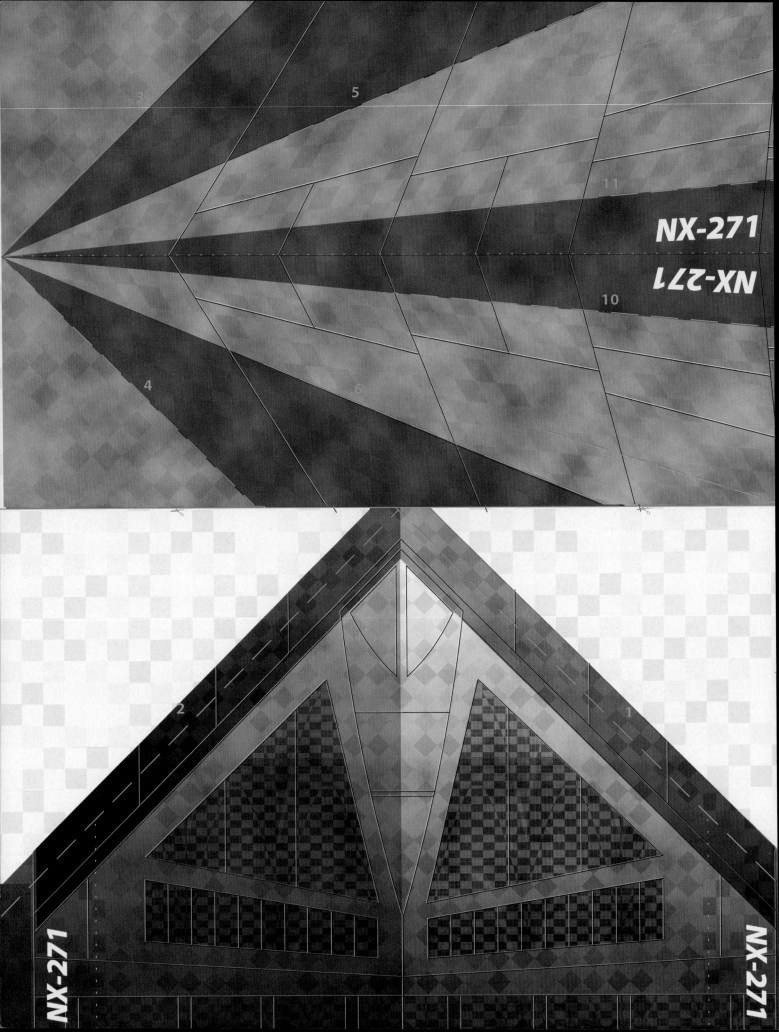

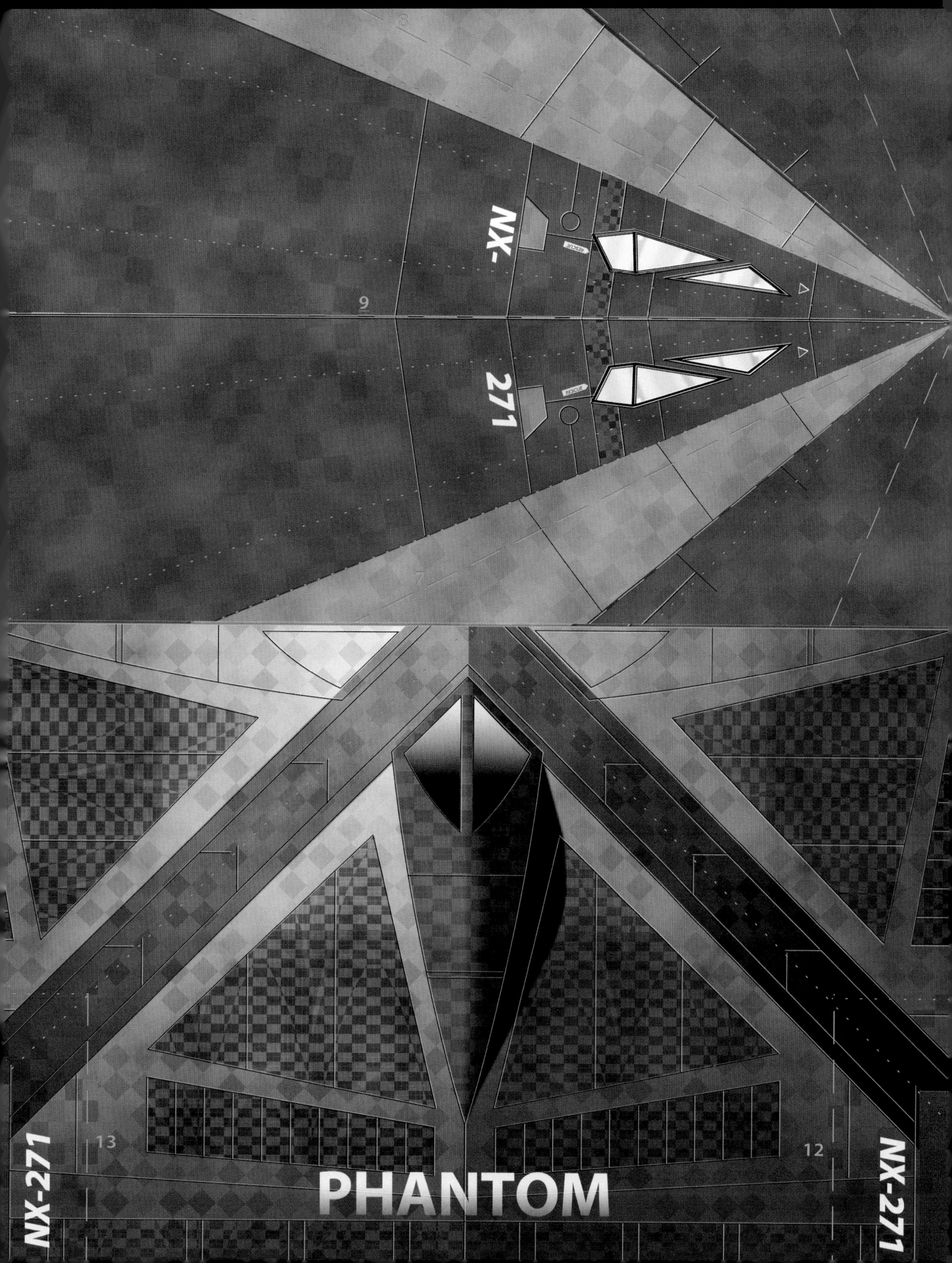

NX-

271

NX-271

NX-271

NX-271

PHANTOM

GALACTICA

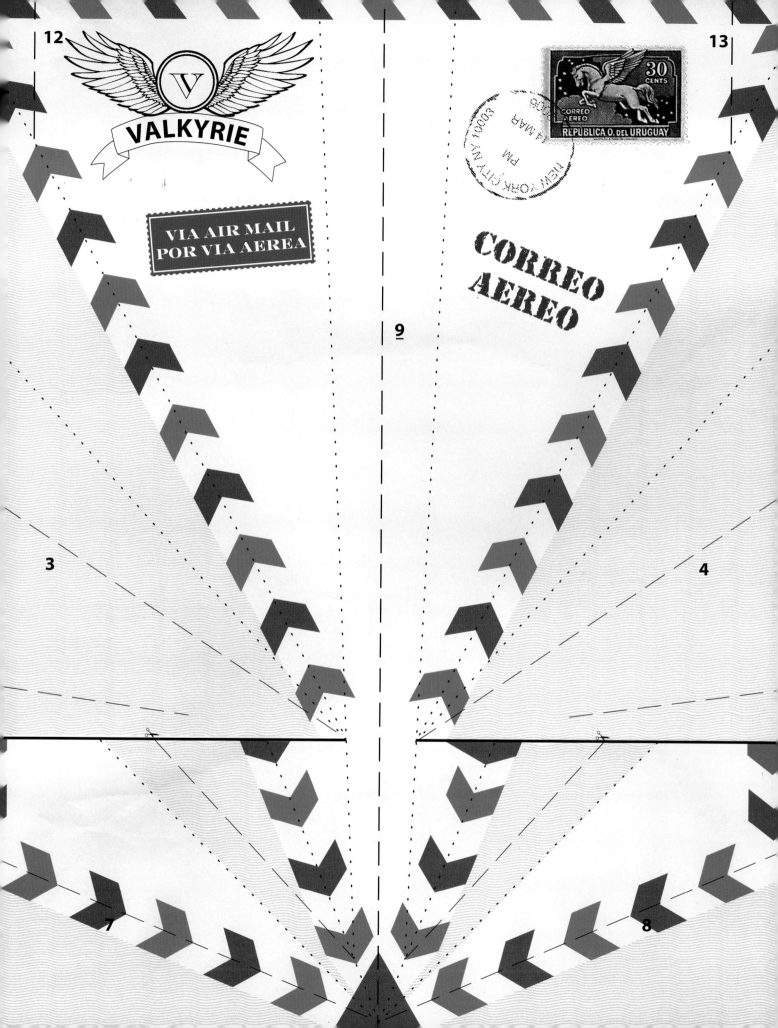

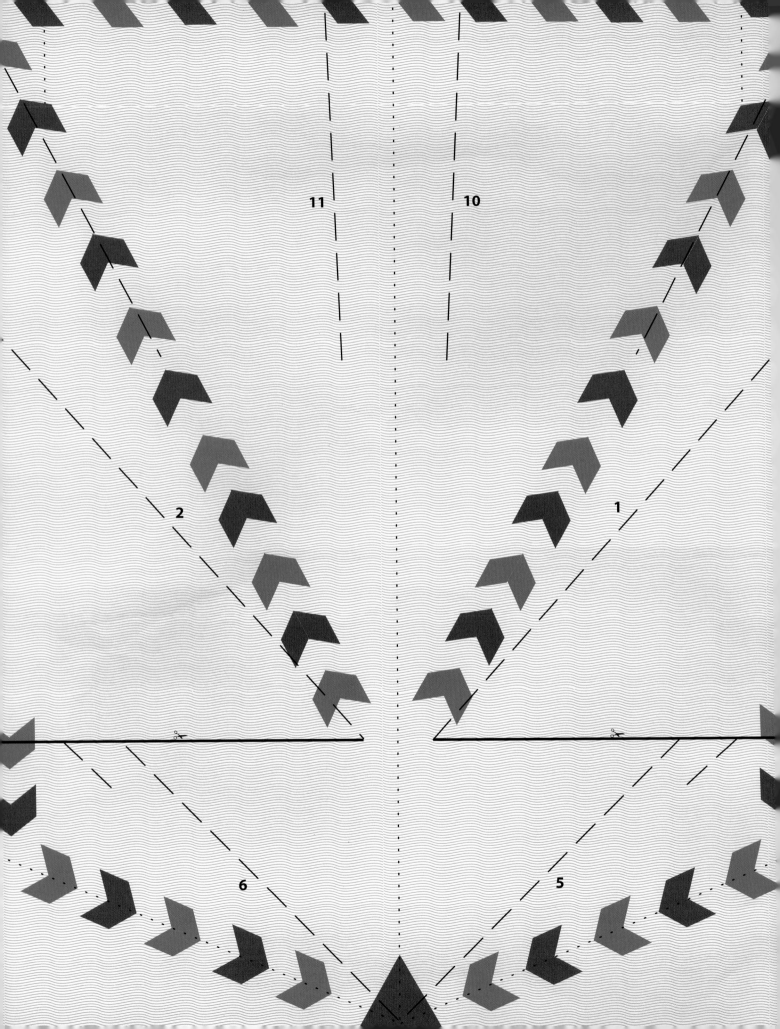

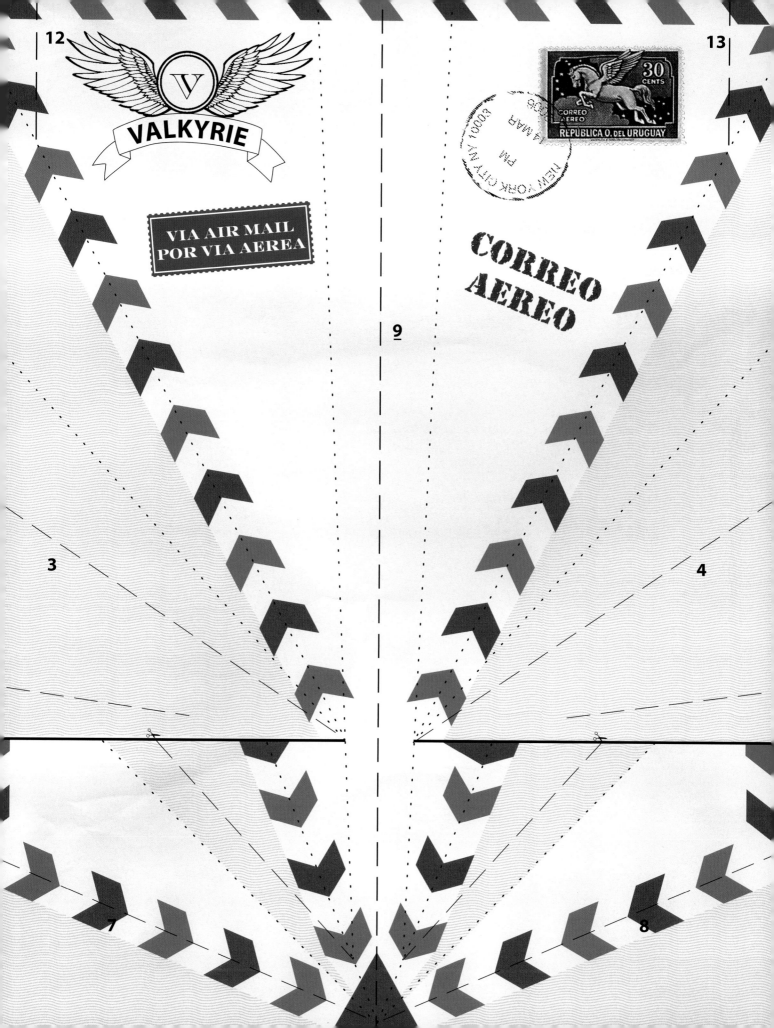

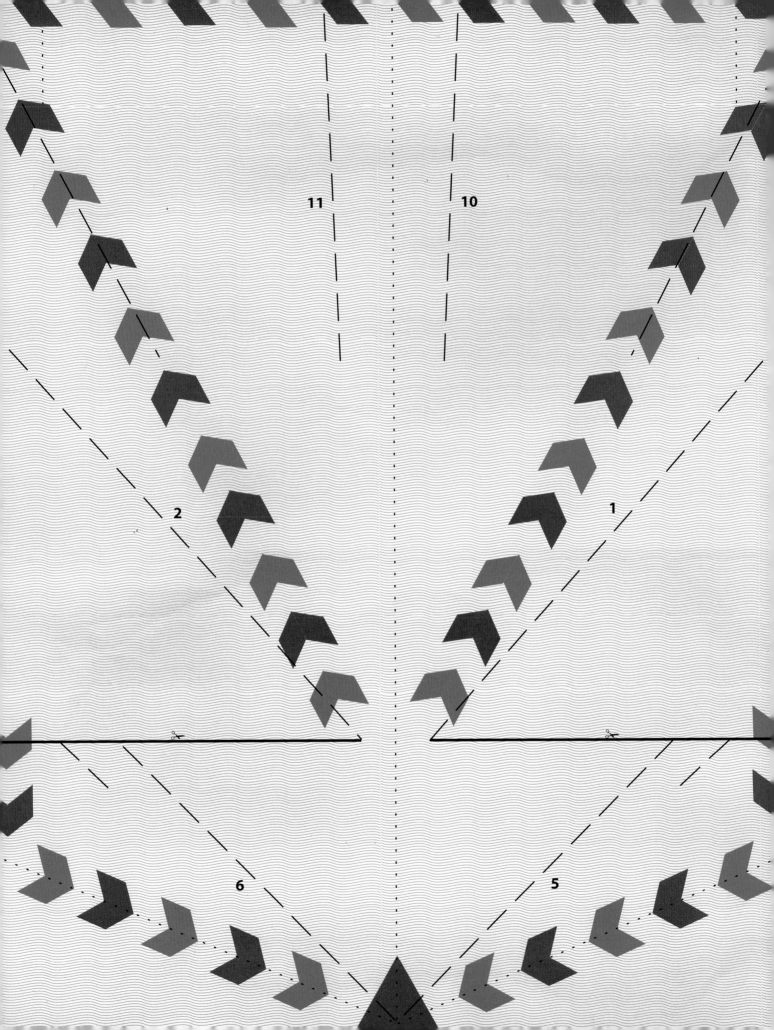

FALCON

Roll tightly

FALCON

4

3

2

1

7

6

Roll tightly

FALCON

4

3

2

1

7

6

FALCON

Roll tightly

STILETTO

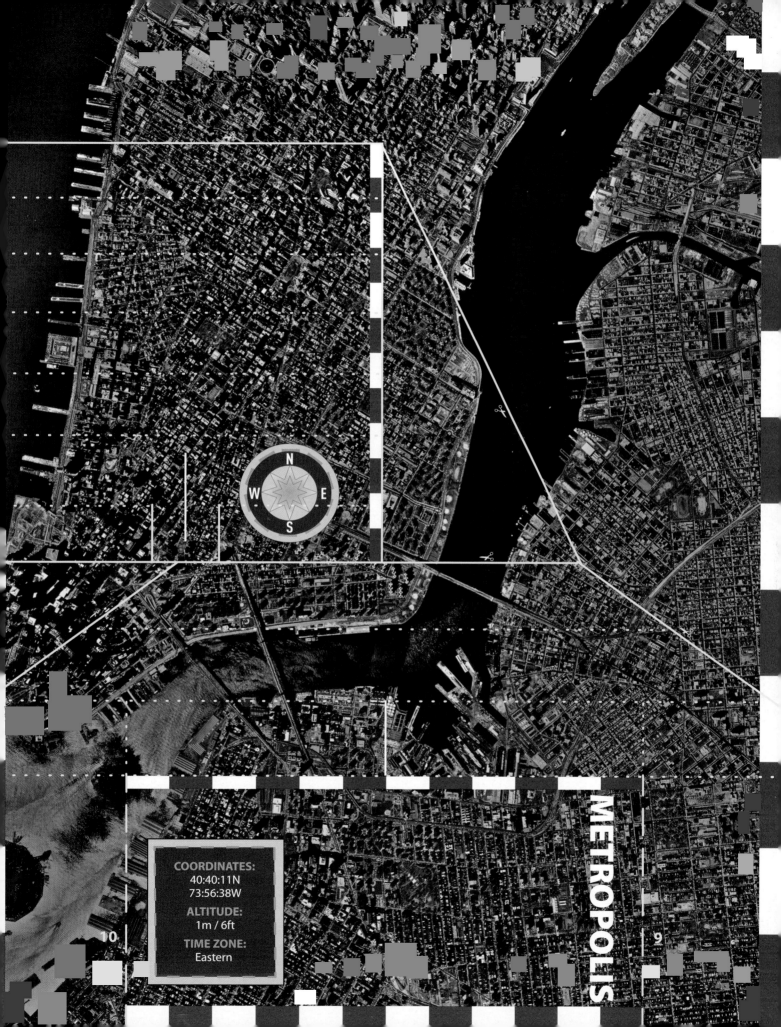

COORDINATES:
40:40:11N
73:56:38W

ALTITUDE:
1m / 6ft

TIME ZONE:
Eastern

METROPOLIS

10

9

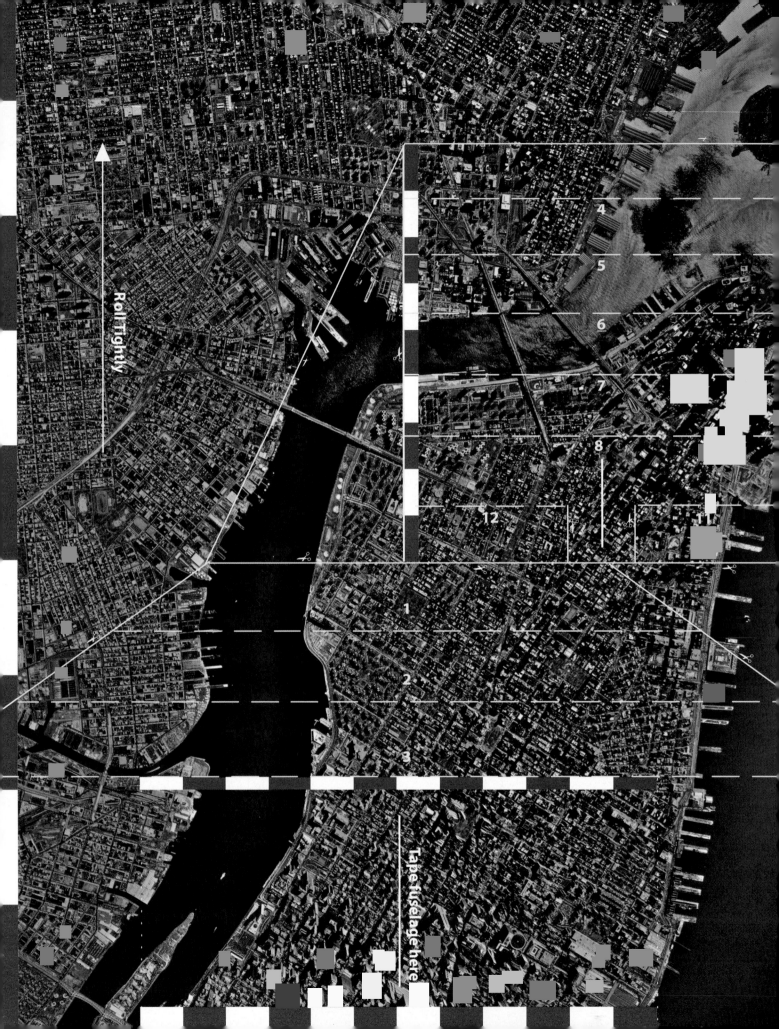

Roll Tightly

Tape fuselage here

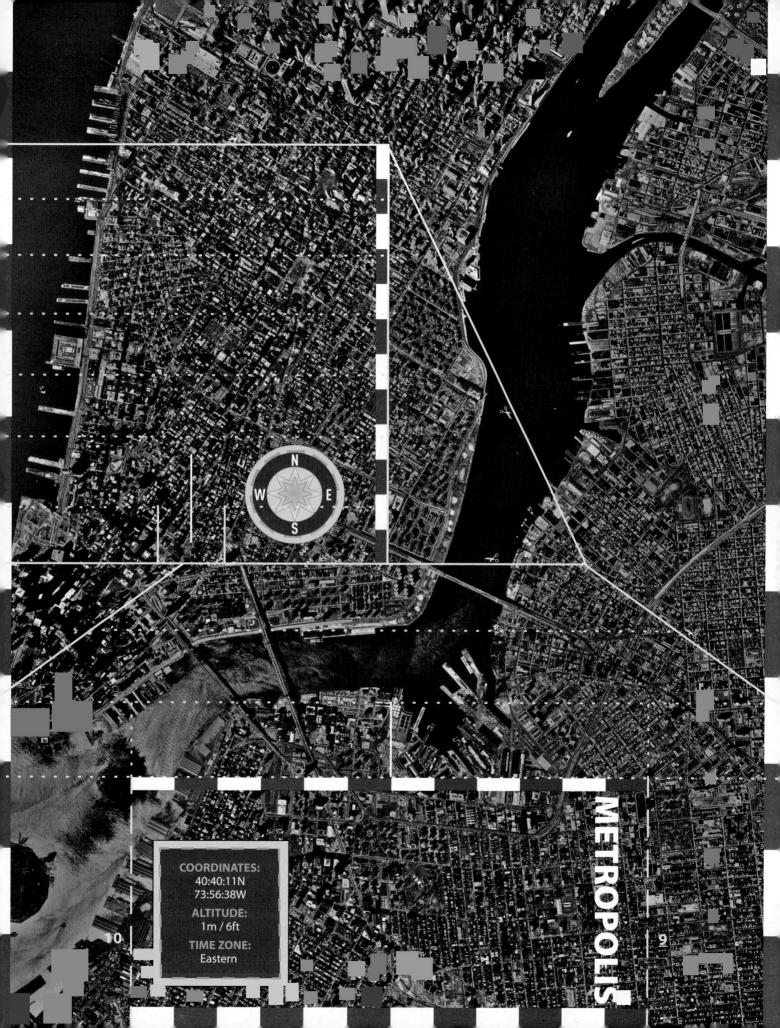

COORDINATES:
40:40:11N
73:56:38W

ALTITUDE:
1m / 6ft

TIME ZONE:
Eastern

METROPOLIS

10

9

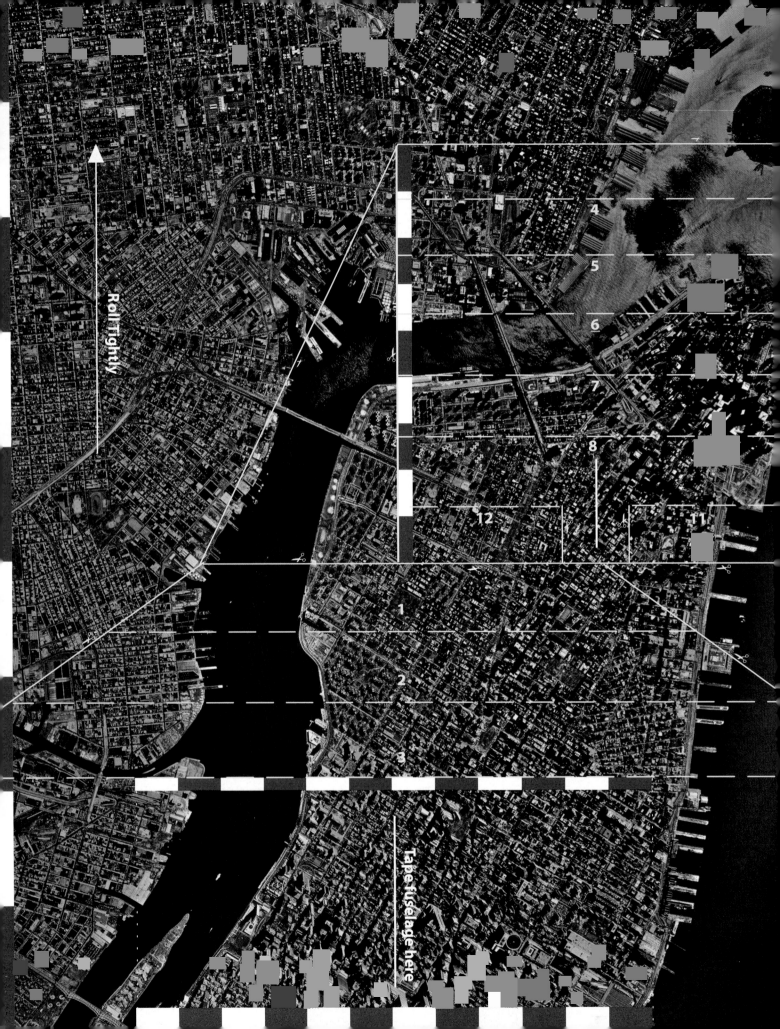

Roll Tightly

Tape fuselage here

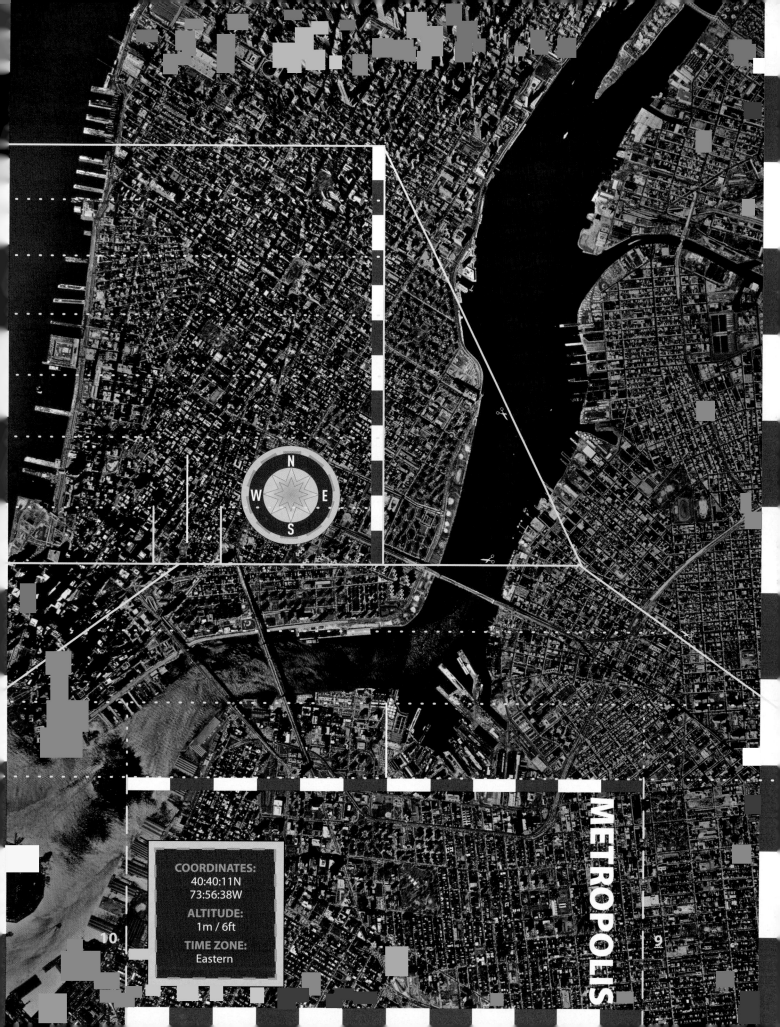

COORDINATES:
40:40:11N
73:56:38W

ALTITUDE:
1m / 6ft

TIME ZONE:
Eastern

METROPOLIS

N
W   E
S

10

9

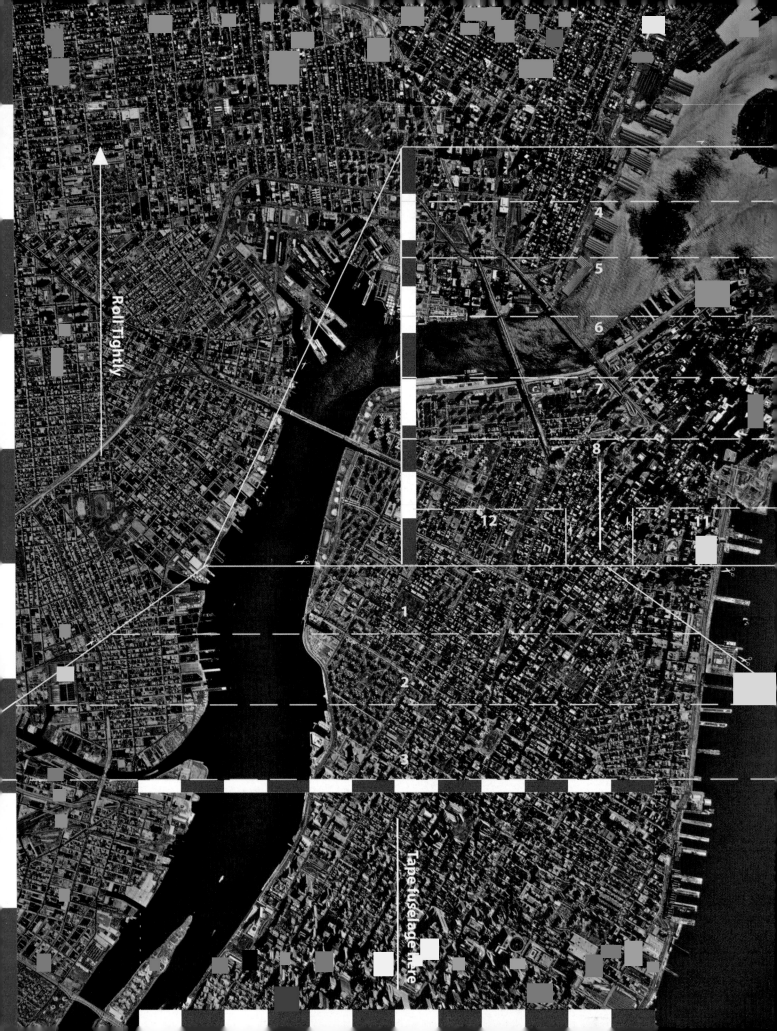

Roll Tightly

Tape fuselage here

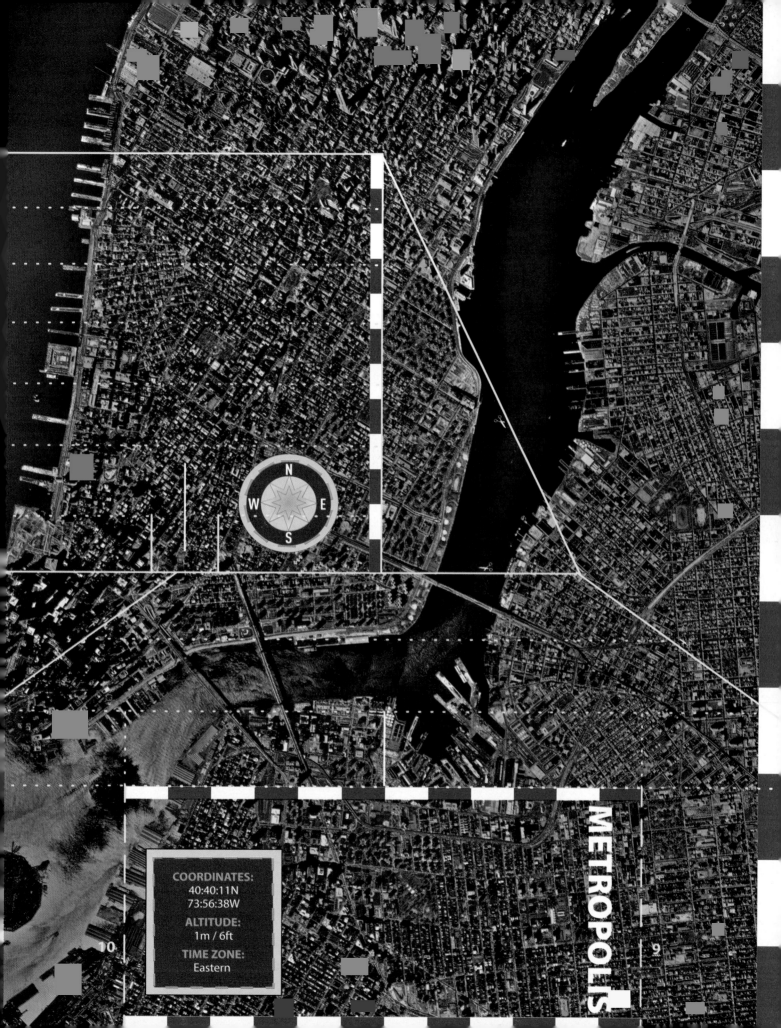

COORDINATES:
40:40:11N
73:56:38W

ALTITUDE:
1m / 6ft

TIME ZONE:
Eastern

METROPOLIS

10

9

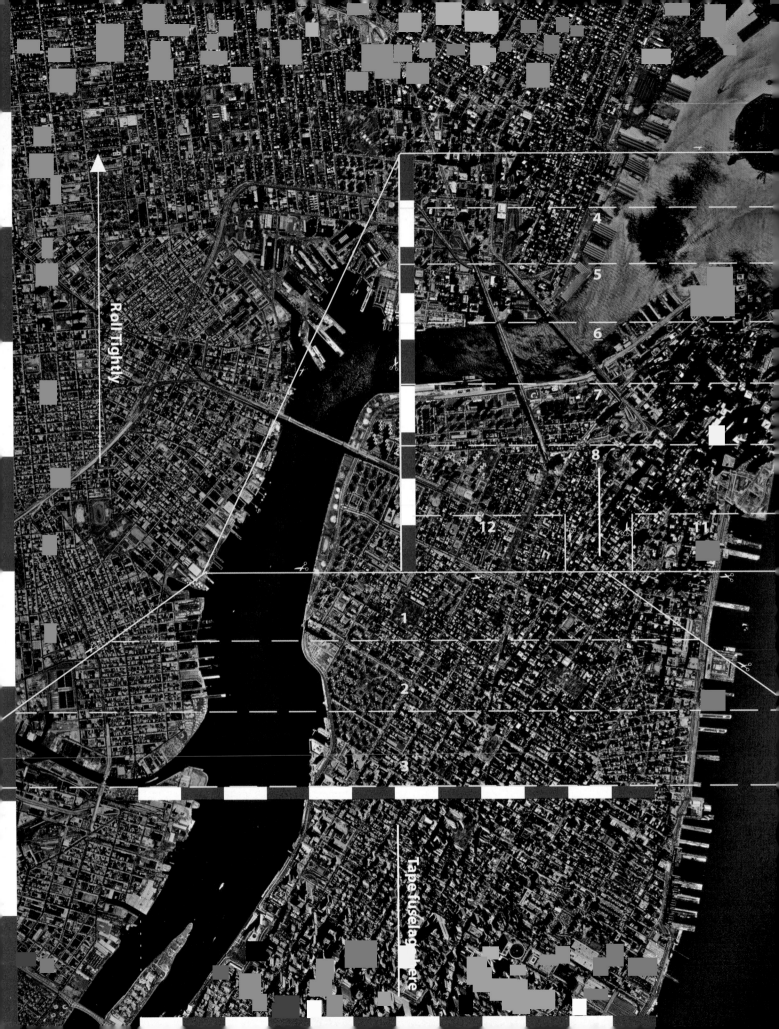

Roll Tightly

Tape fuselage here

4
5
6
7
8
12
11
1
2

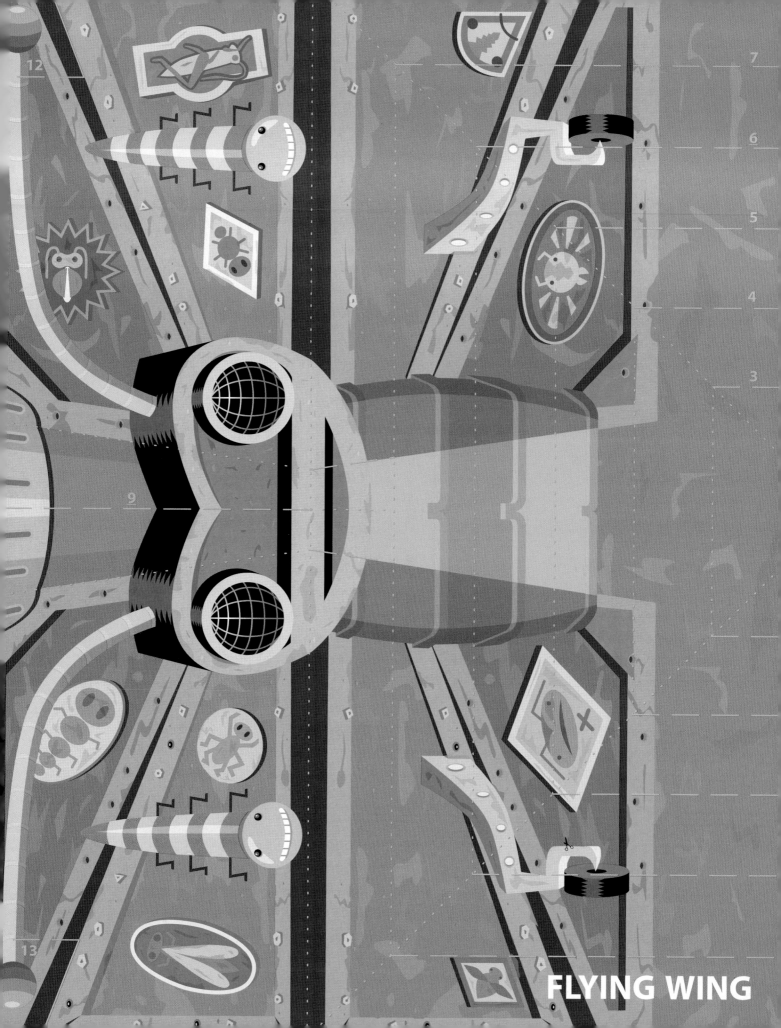

FLYING WING

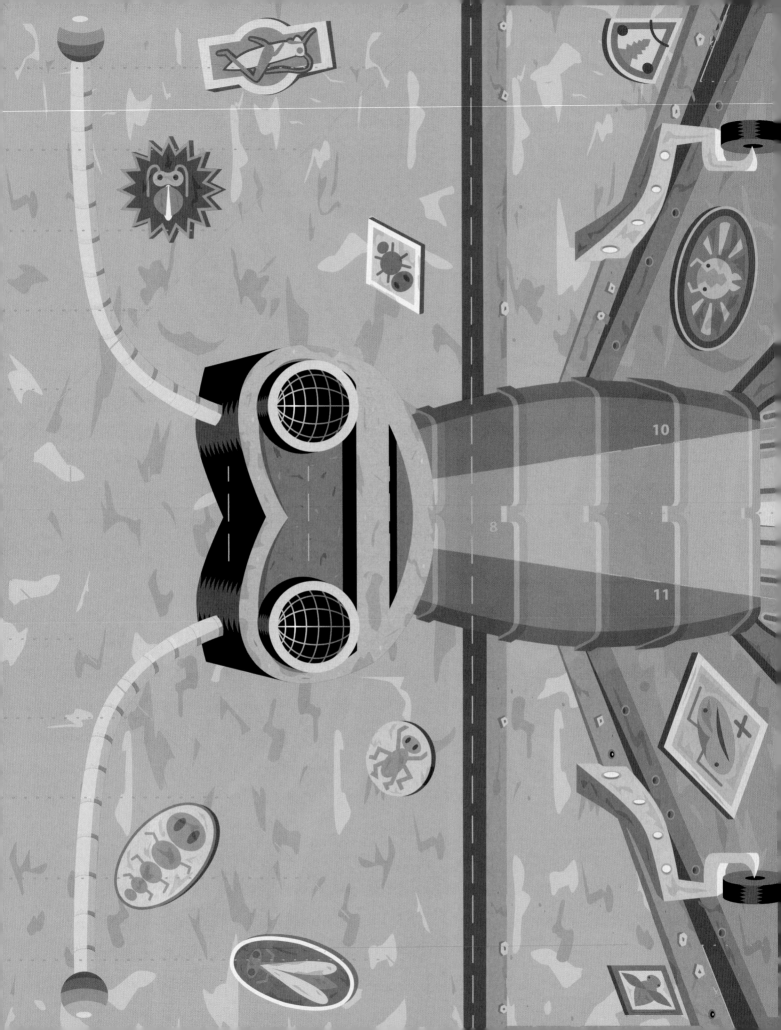

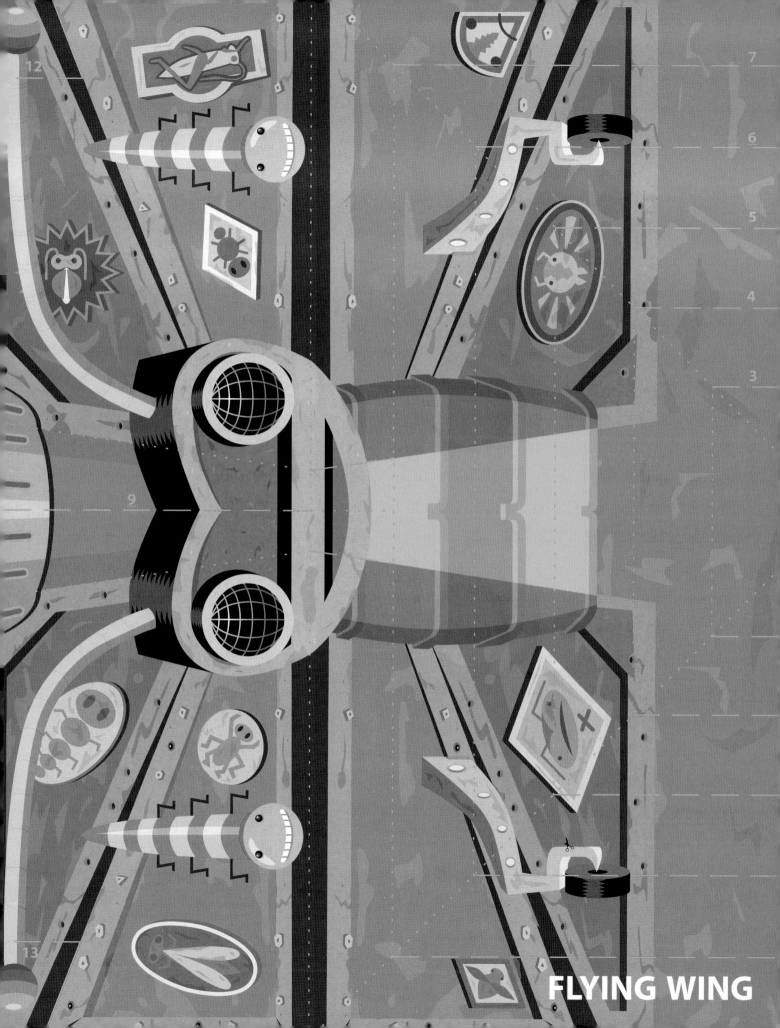

FLYING WING

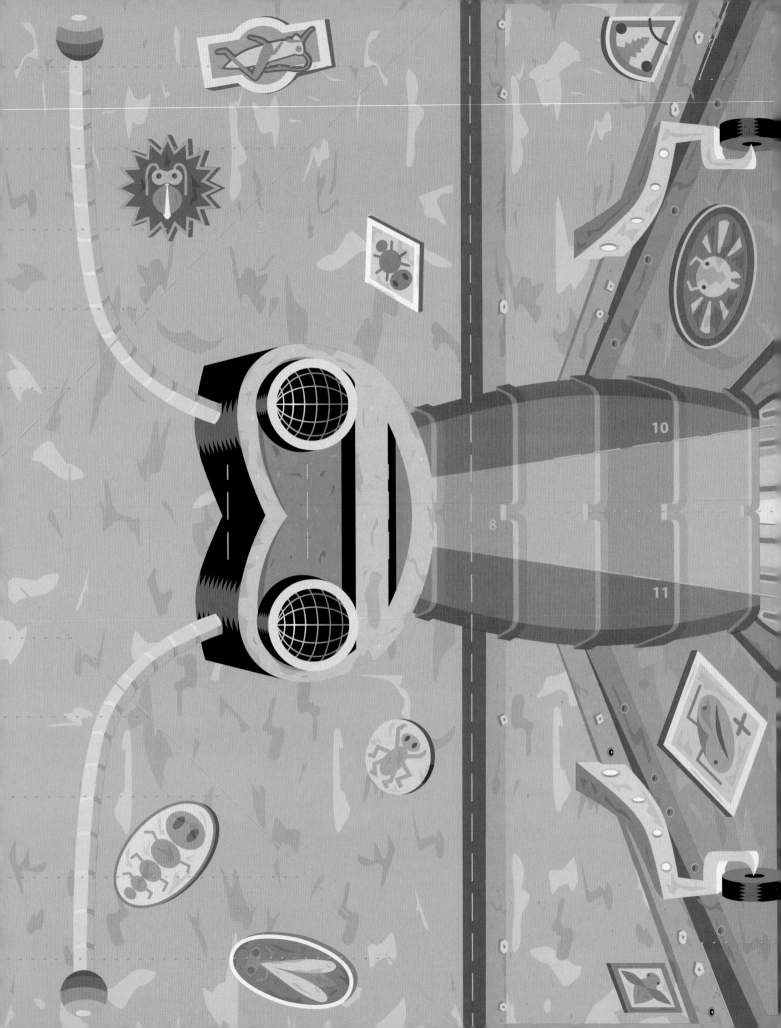

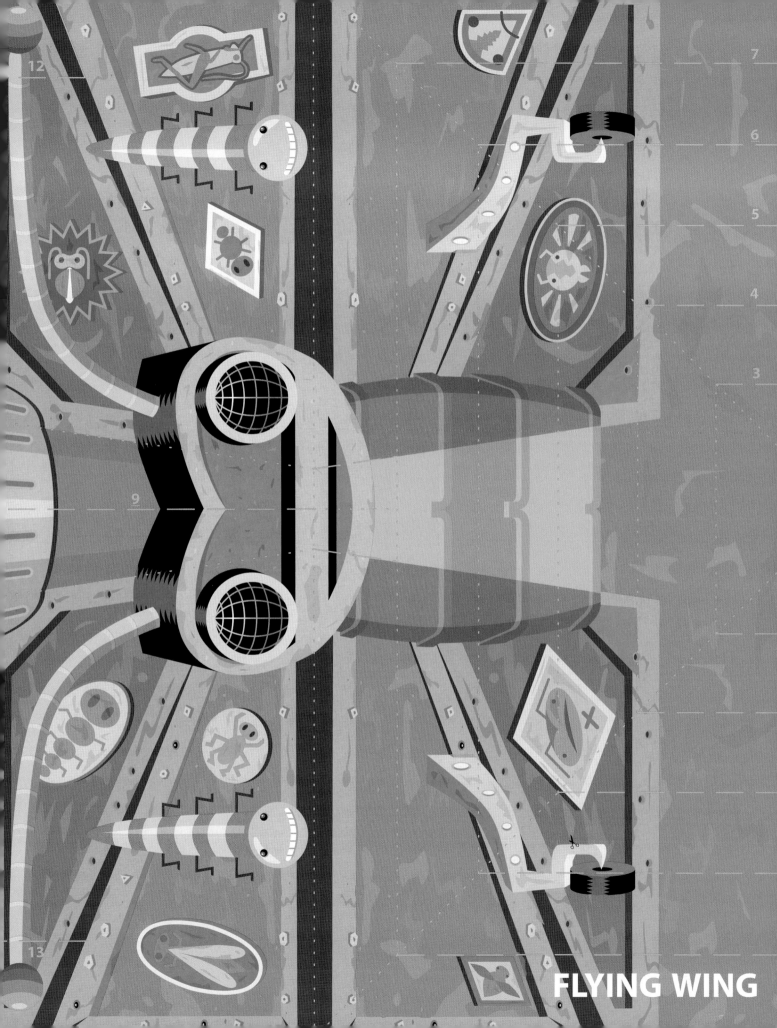

FLYING WING

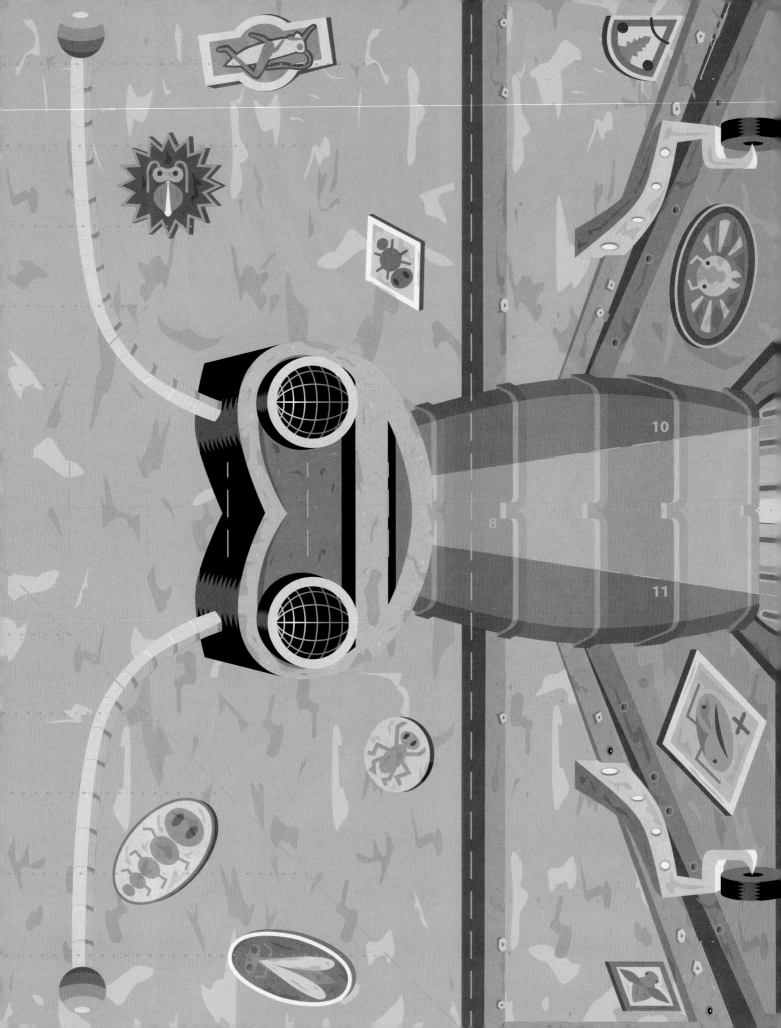

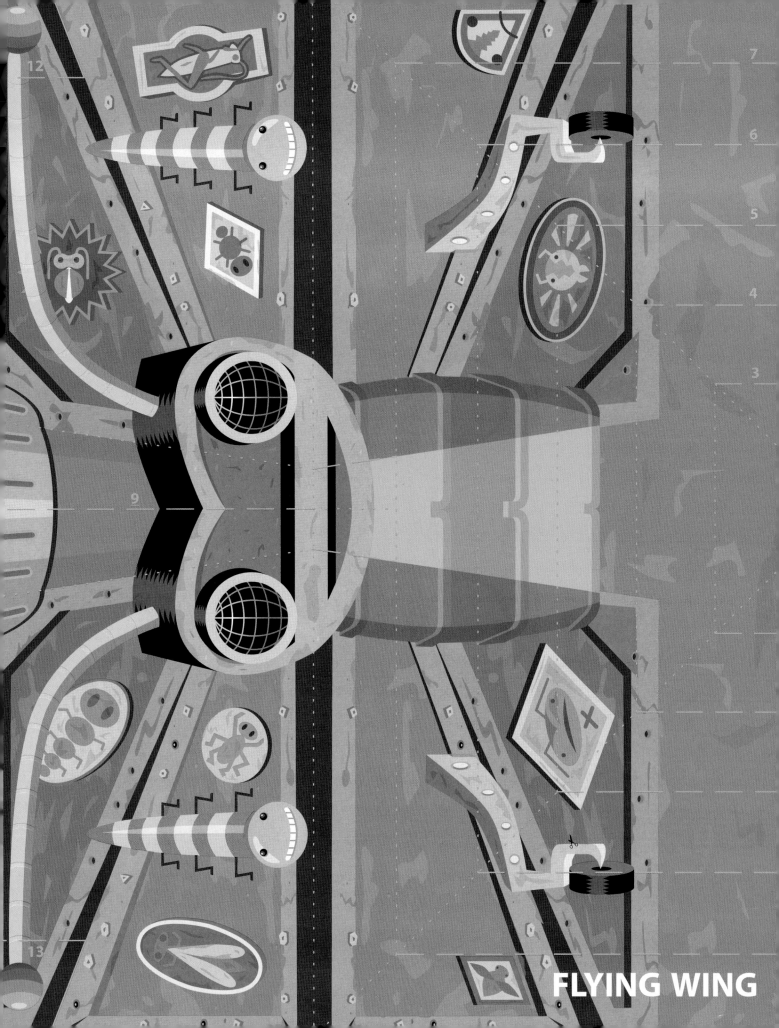

FLYING WING

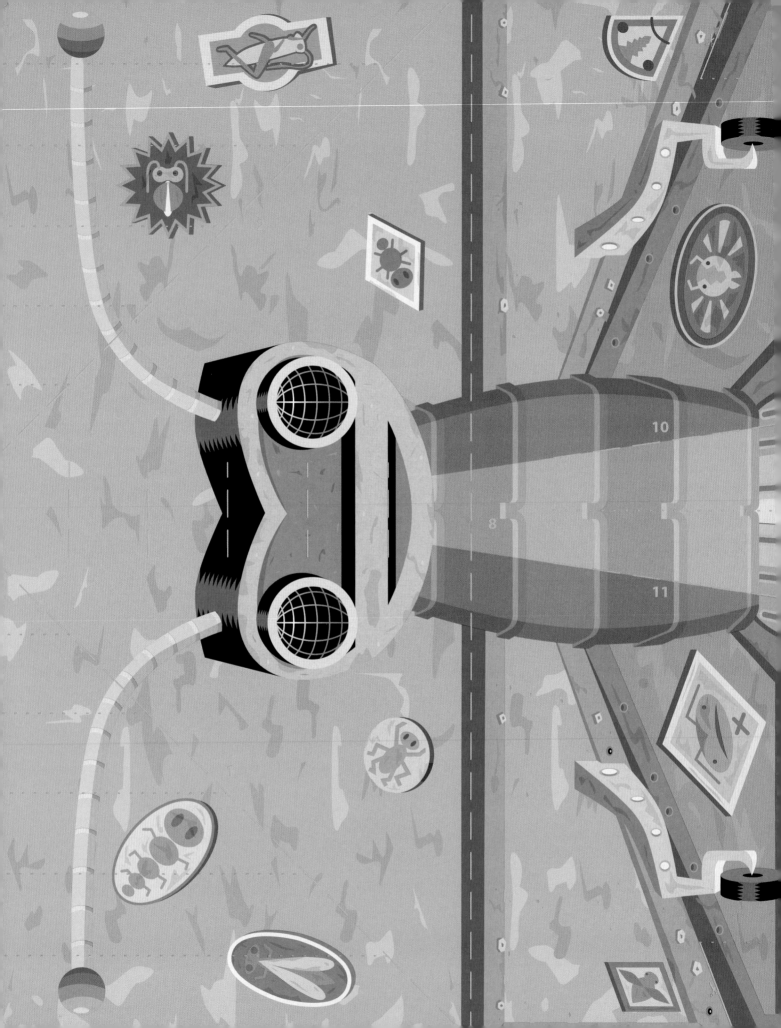

SPITFIRE

SPITFIRE

SPITFIRE